The Cognitive Ability Trainer,
Practice Test and Training Guides for The Grade 6 Cognitive Abilities Test (Level 13/ Form 7)

Not Just a Practice Test! Over 9,000 words on how to answer each problem

by Dustin Pack

Polemics Math

Polemics Math

Polemics Applications LLC produces educational books and apps for the iPhone, iPad and Android platforms. If you enjoy the content of this book feel free to look us up at www.polemicsmath.com. You'll find free content updated weekly and other materials to train in common core math and gifted & talented programs.

If you find a mistake, we would love to fix it.
If you have comments or have trouble with a question
please send email to **info@polemicsmath.com**

This training guide has an iPhone and iPad Companion App! Train on the go with the Cognitive Ability Trainer:

http://bit.ly/COGAT_6

Introduction

The struggle is what matters; this book is not just a practice test to toss at a child. It is a training guide. The language of all of our explanations, tips and tricks have a parental tone. To get maximum effect work through this book's sample tests and then review the answers together. Our appendices in the back not only tell you the answer but how to get to the answer. In all of these areas we are training the student's ability to think critically about each problem.

This book covers the nine categories of questions that your child will see on the grade school CogAT® tests. The material in this book is original in design and modeled after practice tests available online and from feedback from many forum discussions. In certain instances, we have increased the difficulty of the questions beyond the grade level of the student. The important lesson here is for the child to practice struggling with questions. The application of critical thinking in the face of uncertainty is a mainstay of all gifted and talented testing.

To test your child, simply take a sheet of scratch paper and have them mark the answers to each question. The answers to the questions are in the back of the book. As a bonus, for each visual type question we will redisplay the question and explain how you get to the correct answer. Good luck!

Be sure to check out Appendix F for some fun lessons on how to improve critical thinking.

Our objectives for the student:

✓ Gain confidence through practice and review of each problem
✓ Learn how trick-questions are made and how to beat them
✓ Increase critical thinking skills for lifelong use

Table of Contents

Each part of this book contains a full-length quiz on the subjects you'll find in the actual COGAT test. We have separated the sections into three broad categories: Visual Analysis, Language Skills and Numeric Skills. Each section has three different areas to test. At the end of each test is an answer key. We recommend you go through the tests writing answers on a piece of paper and then check your work with the answer key.

The appendices in this book are to help train you for certain material on the test. In appendix A-C we actually repeat every question found on the test and tell you how to get to the right answer. In Appendix D and E we will show you the tips and tricks to the number type questions. Appendix F is a set of essays on how to think critically and achieve the best scores on the exam.

Visual Analysis

Visual Analysis

This book is best used as a training guide. When it comes to visual analysis and pattern recognition it is important to make distinctions on different levels. For example, is the pattern presented color based? Shape based? Or number based? Maybe a little of each?

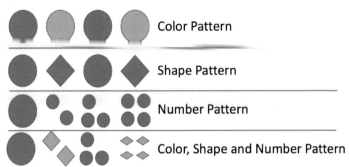

Color Pattern

Shape Pattern

Number Pattern

Color, Shape and Number Pattern

Sometimes shapes will rotate or turn in a question. This is an important clue to the right answer.

 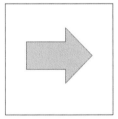  

Sometimes the pictures have a lot of **noise.** This is when there are parts of a picture that are just there to confuse you. In this sample what is consistent in each picture? It's the blue heart. All of those other shapes are there to mislead you. While everything may be a clue to the answer some parts of the picture are really there just as a distraction.

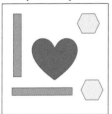 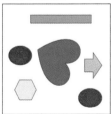 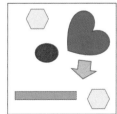 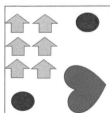

Visual Analysis: Figure Classification

In Figure **Classification** you are going to be looking at three pictures and you will think about how they are familiar. Maybe each picture has the same colors or shapes or they are arranged in a certain way. Find what is common among all the pictures. Then pick an answer that has the most common features of the three pictures presented. There is often more than one thing in common so be sure to study the pictures in many ways before answering the question.

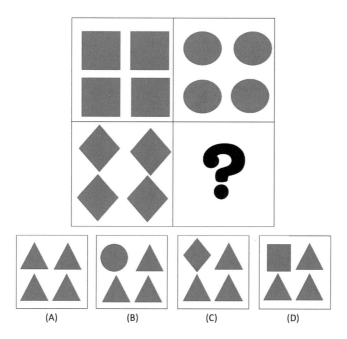

Here is a simple example. In this series of pictures, you see each one has four shapes that are all the same type. The classification is "All shapes in the picture are of the same kind", Answer A shows four triangles. All other answers do not show four of the same shape.

WARNING: These are meant to be hard! It's ok to miss these as long as you are practicing looking for common features among the shapes.

Figure Classification: Question 1

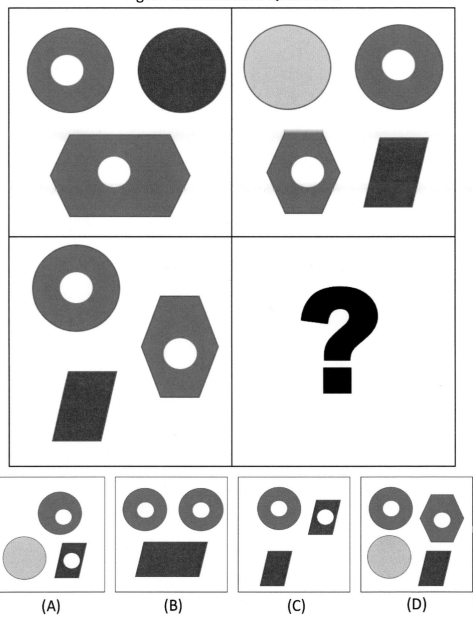

(A) (B) (C) (D)

Figure Classification: Question 2

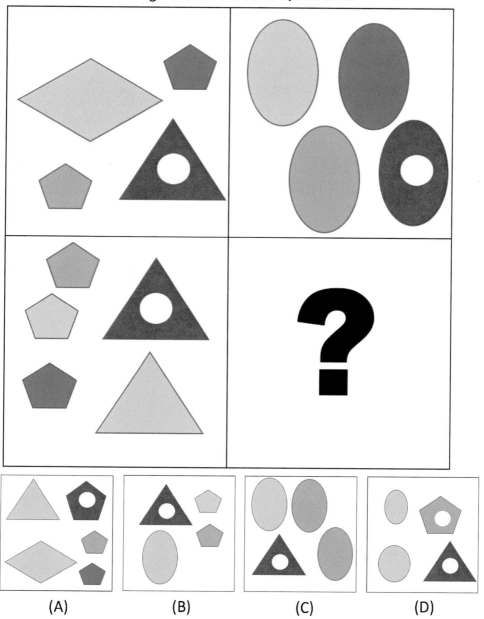

Figure Classification: Question 3

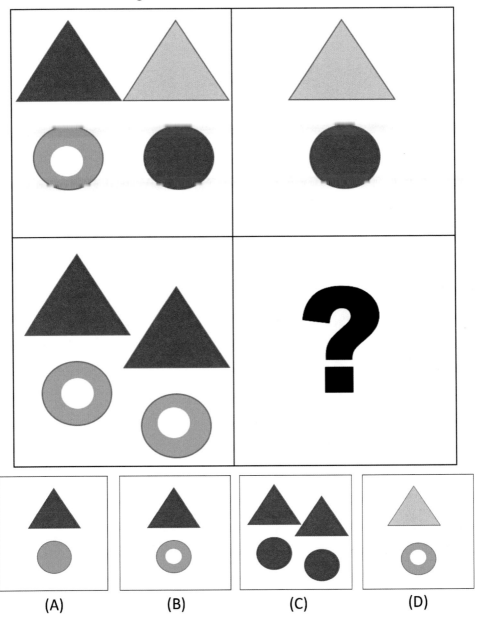

(A)   (B)   (C)   (D)

Figure Classification: Question 4

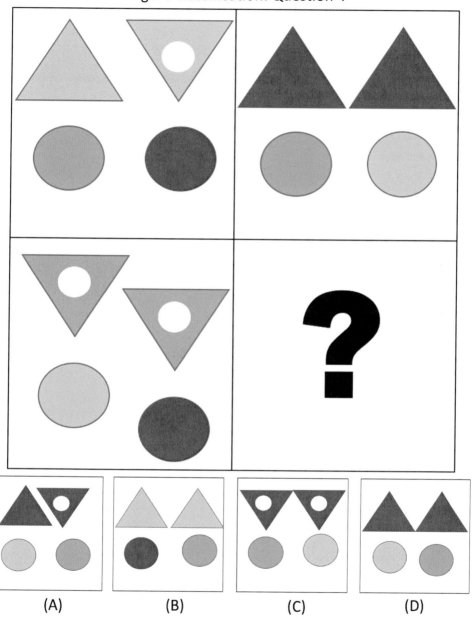

(A)   (B)   (C)   (D)

Figure Classification: Question 5

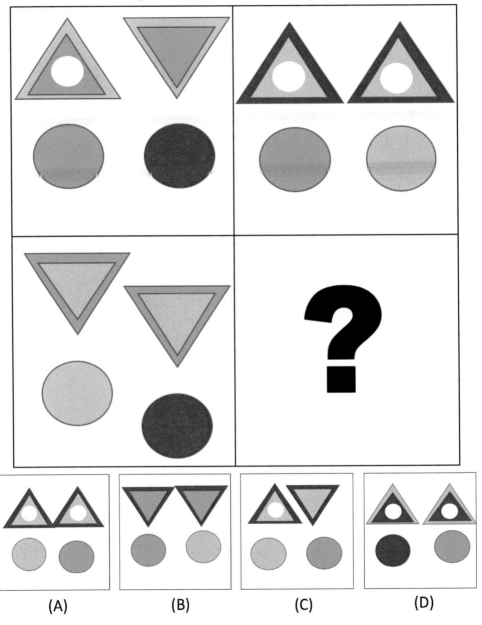

(A) (B) (C) (D)

Figure Classification: Question 6

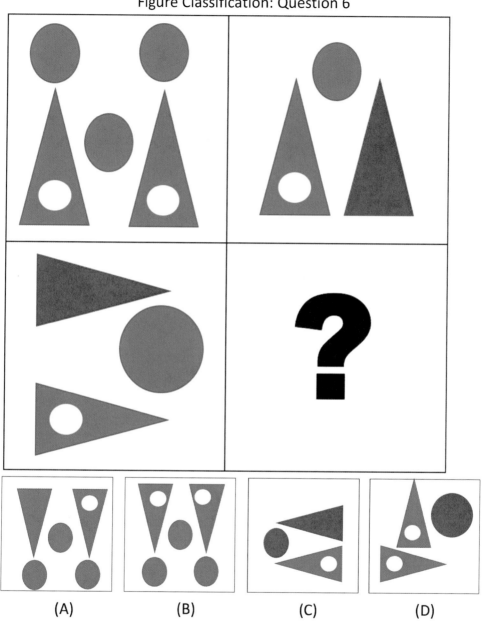

(A) (B) (C) (D)

Figure Classification: Question 7

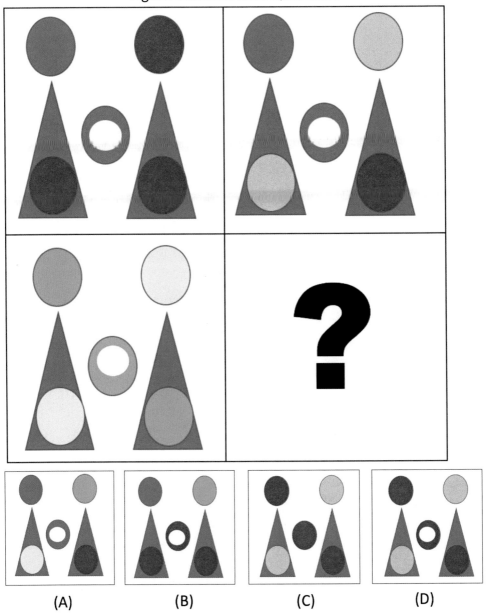

(A) (B) (C) (D)

Figure Classification: Question 8

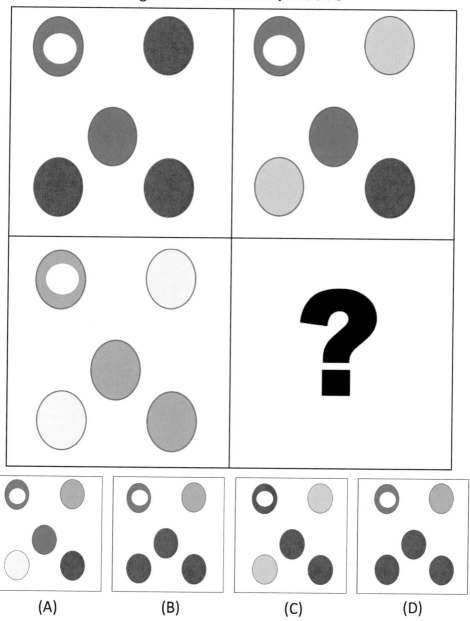

Figure Classification: Question 9

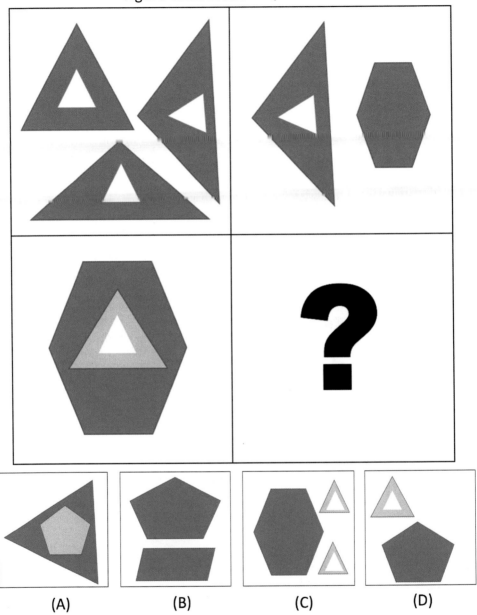

(A) (B) (C) (D)

Figure Classification: Question 10

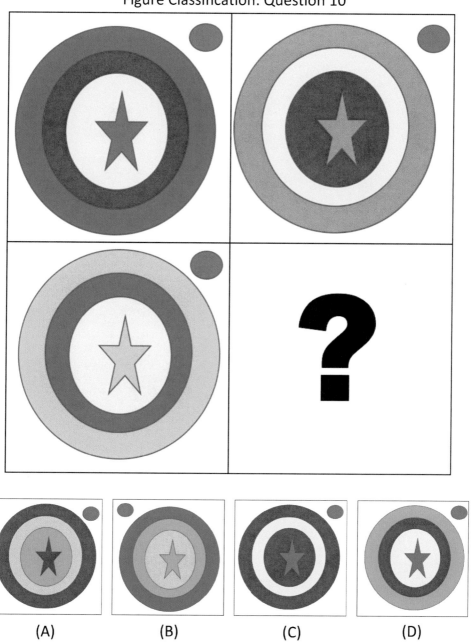

(A)   (B)   (C)   (D)

Figure Classification: Question 11

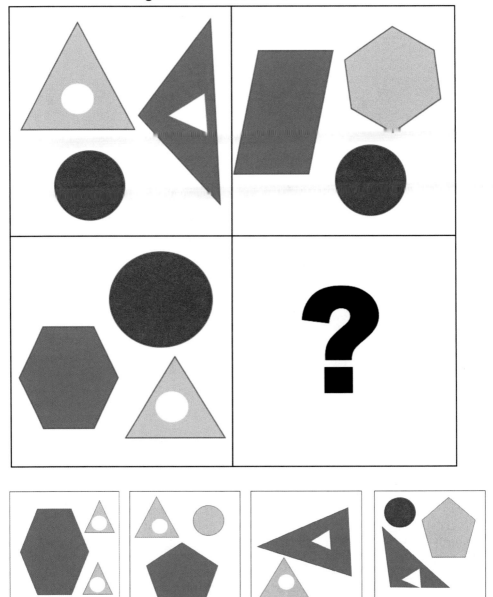

(A) (B) (C) (D)

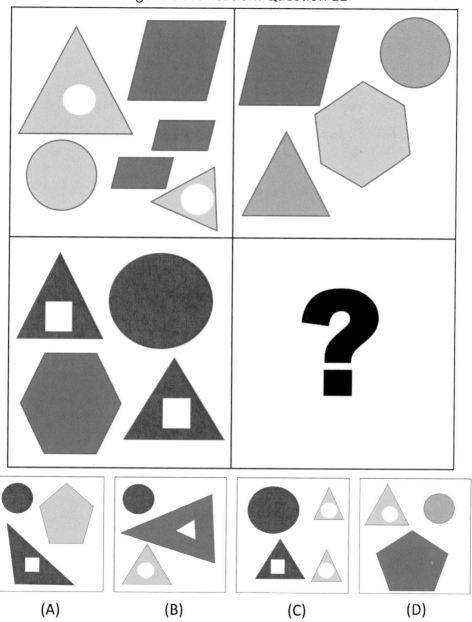

(A)   (B)   (C)   (D)

Figure Classification: Question 13

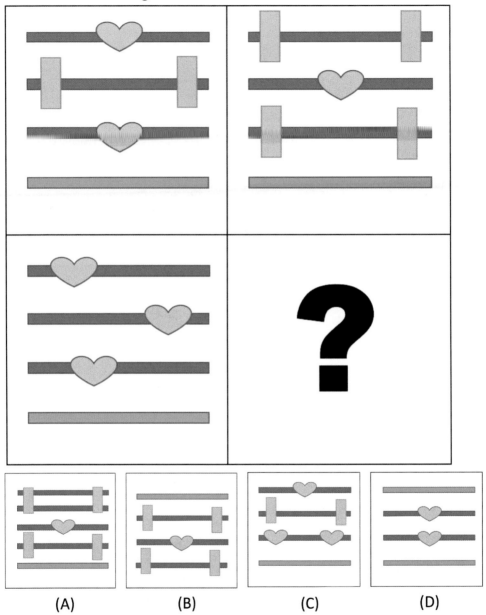

(A)   (B)   (C)   (D)

Figure Classification: Question 14

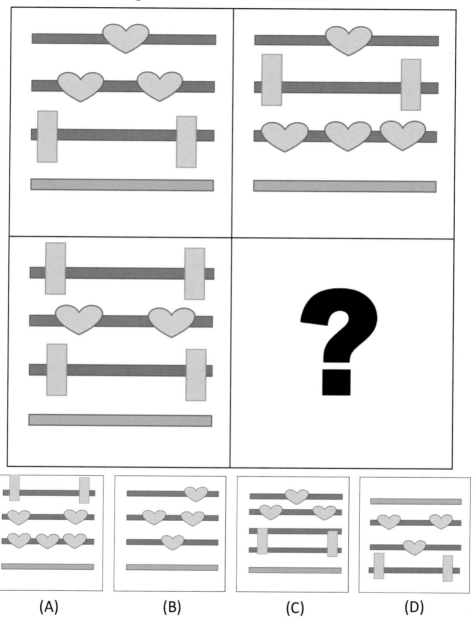

(A) (B) (C) (D)

Figure Classification: Question 15

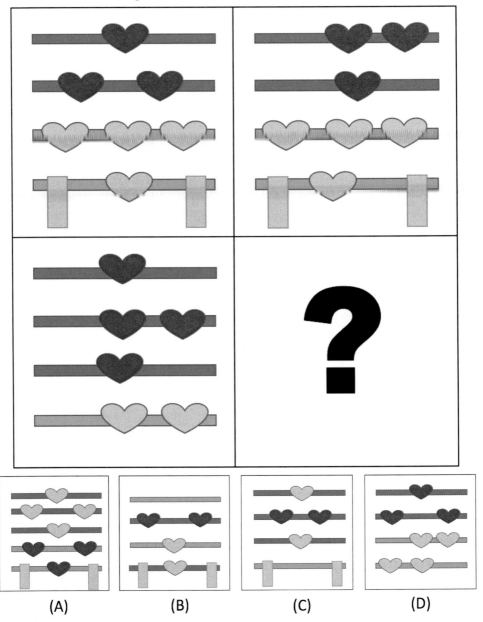

(A)　　　(B)　　　(C)　　　(D)

Figure Classification: Question 16

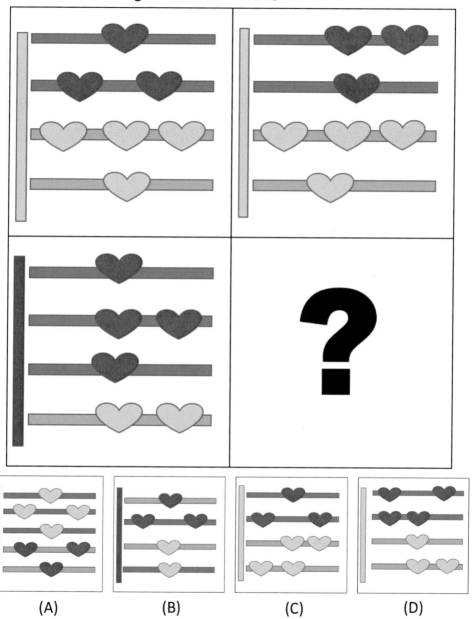

(A)   (B)   (C)   (D)

Figure Classification: Question 17

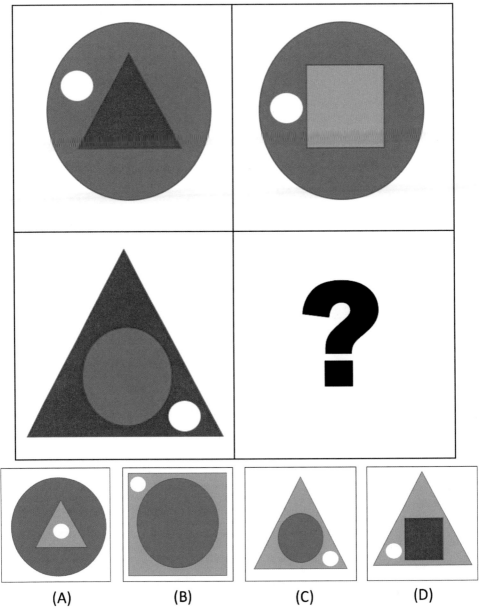

(A) (B) (C) (D)

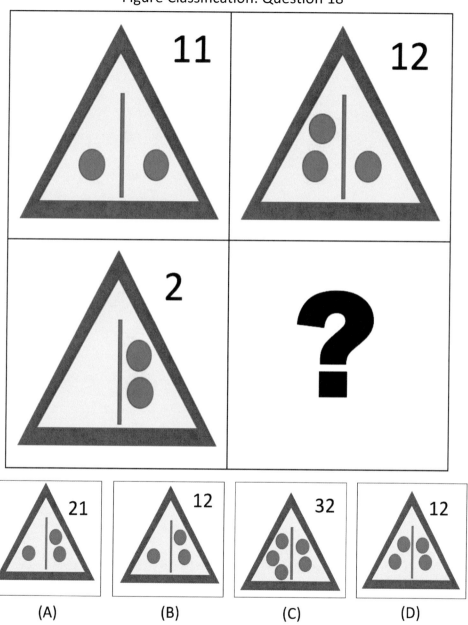

(A)   (B)   (C)   (D)

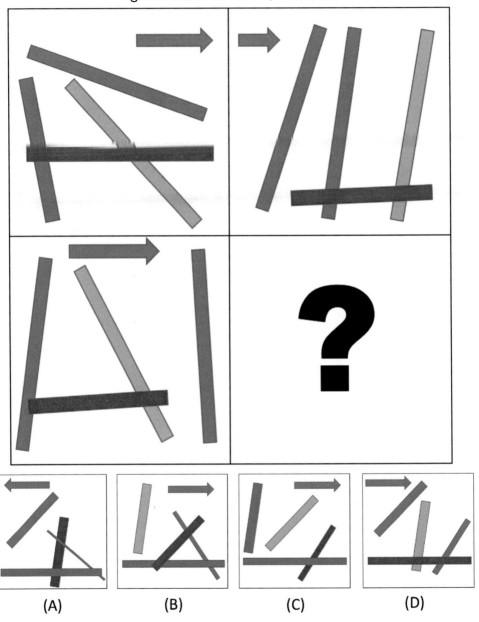

Figure Classification: Question 20

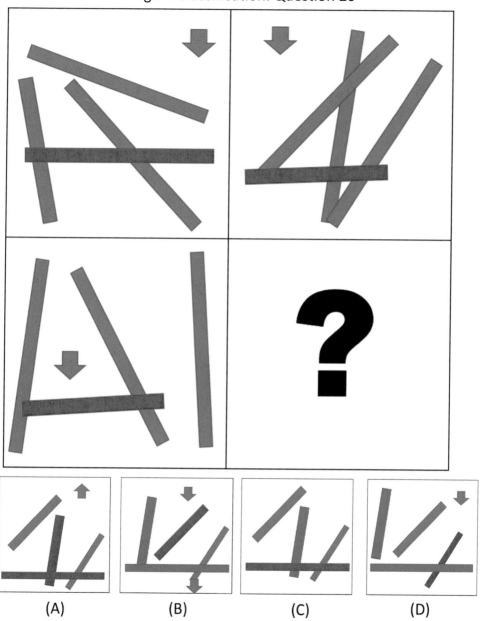

(A) (B) (C) (D)

Figure Classification: Answer Key

Question	Answer
1	D
2	A
3	B
4	D
5	A
6	B
7	D
8	C
9	C
10	A
11	D
12	A
13	C
14	A
15	D
16	C
17	B
18	A
19	D
20	C

Please See Appendix A for a detailed explanation for each of these answers. Appendix A is written for adults to explain to the student how a piece of critical thinking occurred on a problem. Tip: use this review time as a discussion platform on other ways the child may have found the answers.

Visual Analysis: Figure Matrices

The figures in each pattern follow a pattern. The pattern reads from left to right and top to bottom. Pick the next picture to complete the pattern. Ask yourself these questions:
- Do the shapes change size?
- Do the number of shapes go up or down?
- Do the colors of the shapes change?
- Are the shapes on top of each other or separated?
- Did the shapes rotate?
- How many sides does each shape have in the pattern?

Any one or more of these questions can assist you in finding the pattern.

In the below example the top left white box rotates to the left AND changes colors to orange. When looking at this problem we can ask, "What happened to the white box?" Then we can say, "The white box rotated and changed colors to orange." Next we can look at the blue triangle and ask, "What will the blue triangle look like when it rotates and changes color to orange?" The answer is (D). Now practice this thought process on the questions in this section.

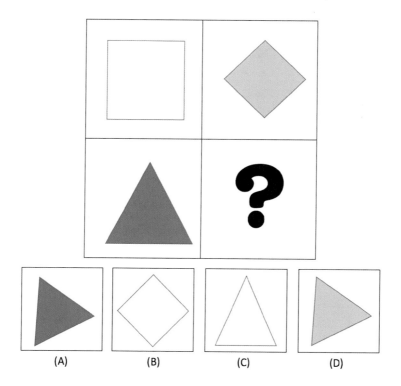

(A)　　　　(B)　　　　(C)　　　　(D)

Figure Matrices: Question 1

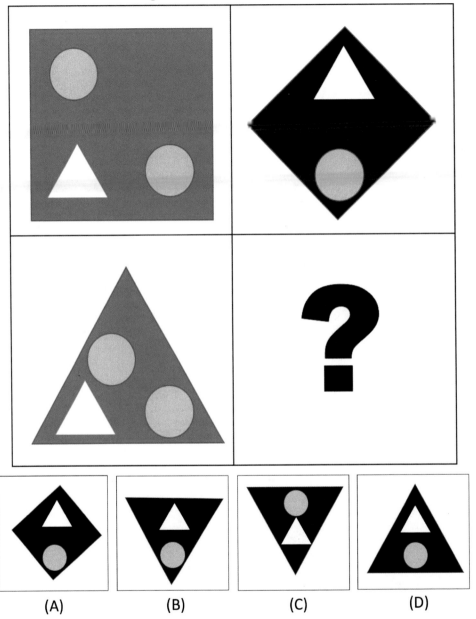

(A) (B) (C) (D)

Figure Matrices: Question 2

(A)   (B)   (C)   (D)

Figure Matrices: Question 3

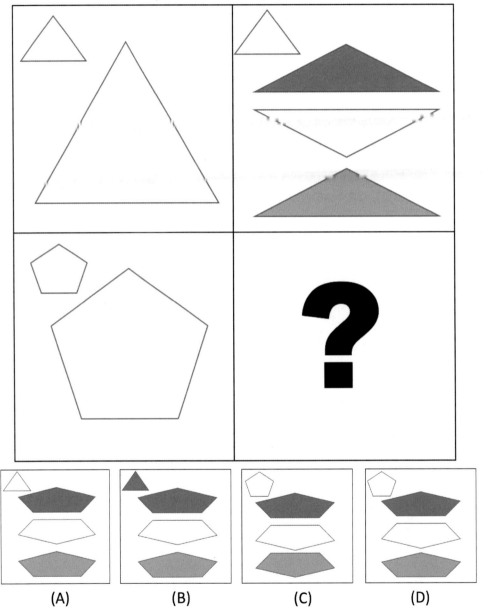

(A)   (B)   (C)   (D)

Figure Matrices: Question 4

(A) (B) (C) (D)

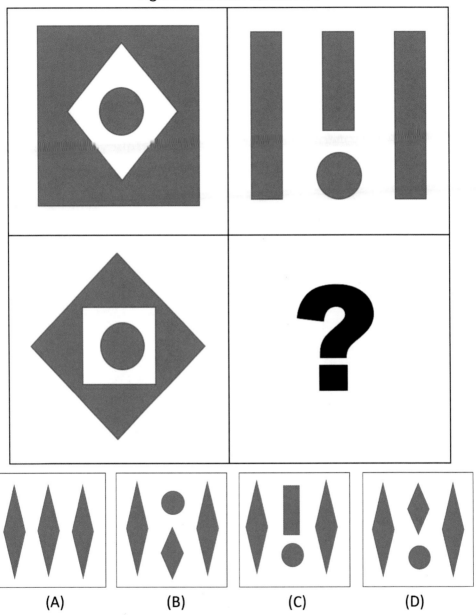

(A) (B) (C) (D)

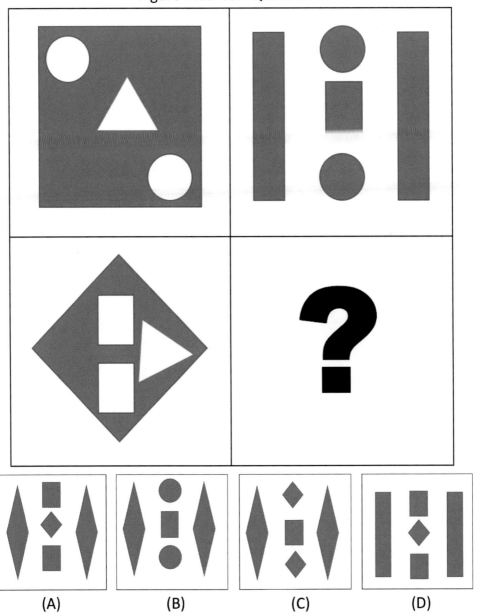

(A)   (B)   (C)   (D)

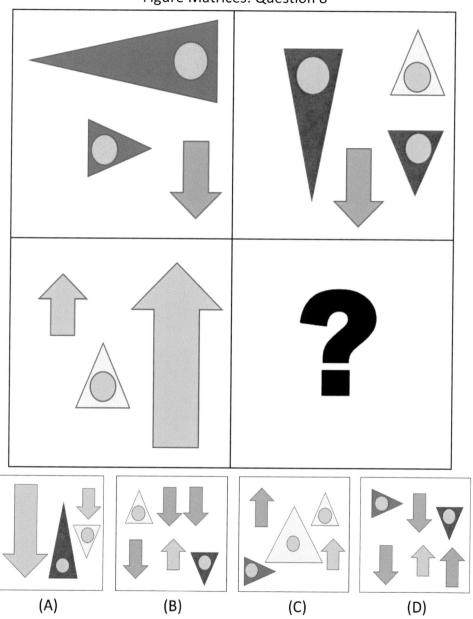

(A)　　　　(B)　　　　(C)　　　　(D)

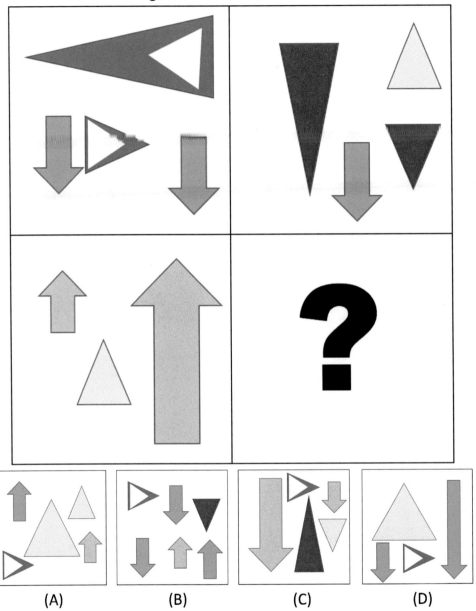

(A)   (B)   (C)   (D)

Figure Matrices: Question 10

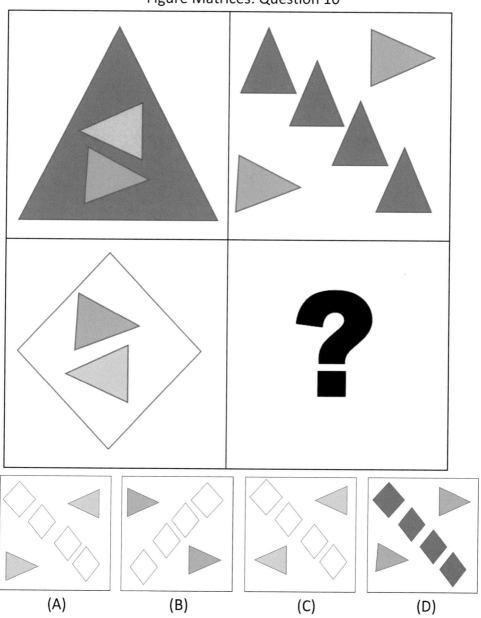

(A) (B) (C) (D)

(A)   (B)   (C)   (D)

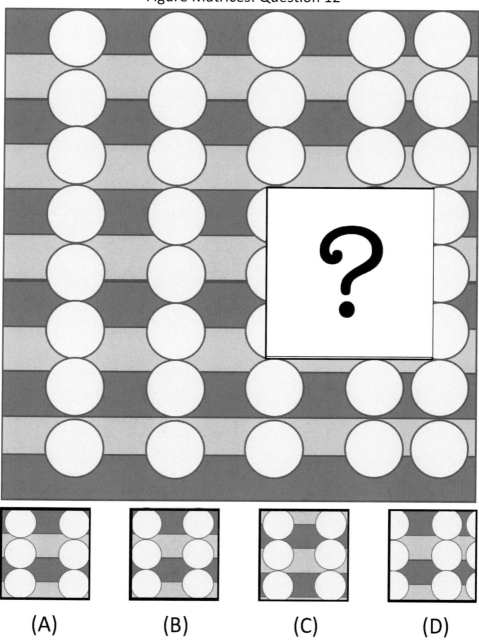

(A)   (B)   (C)   (D)

(A)　　　　　(B)　　　　　(C)　　　　　(D)

(A)　　　　(B)　　　　(C)　　　　(D)

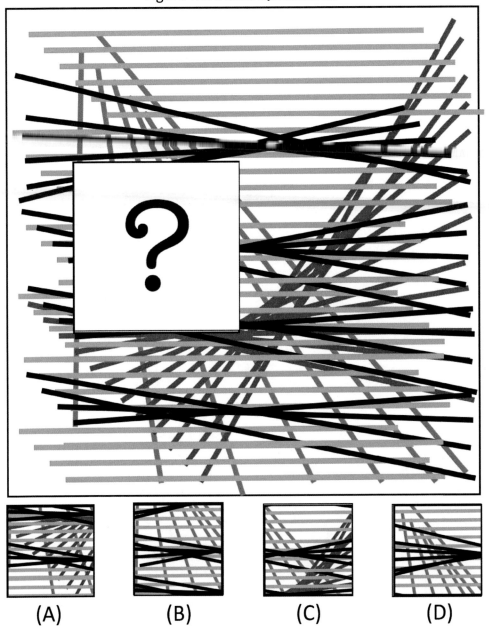

(A)   (B)   (C)   (D)

Figure Matrices: Question 17

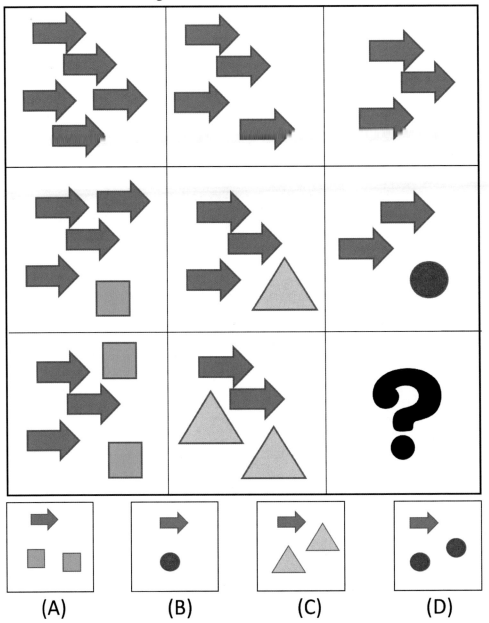

Figure Matrices: Question 18

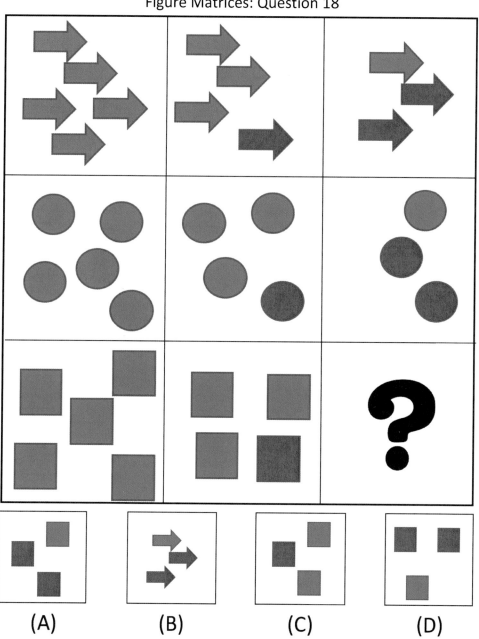

(A) (B) (C) (D)

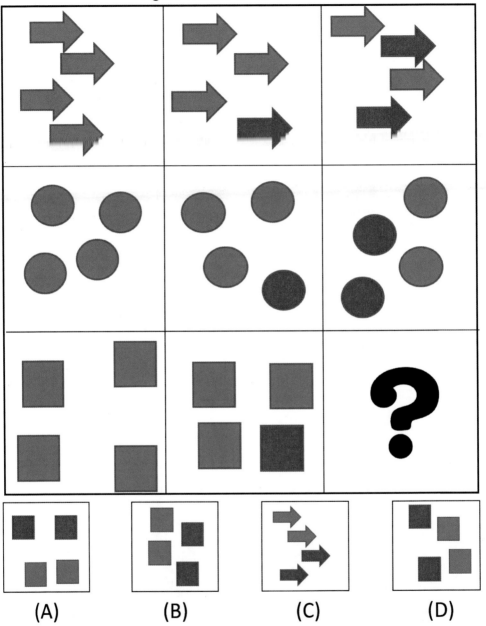

Figure Matrices: Question 20

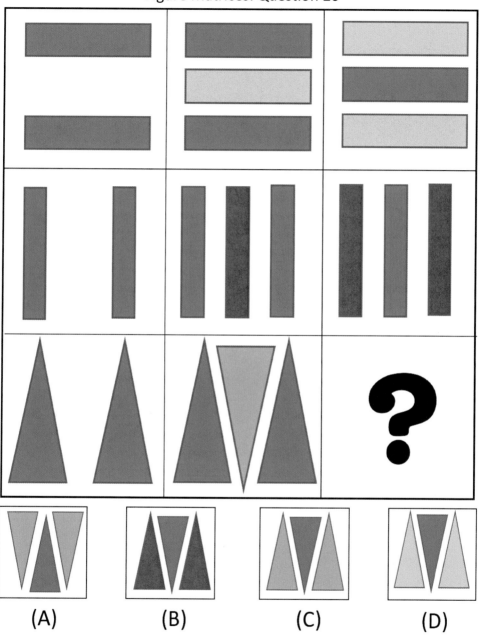

(A)   (B)   (C)   (D)

Figure Matrices: Question 21

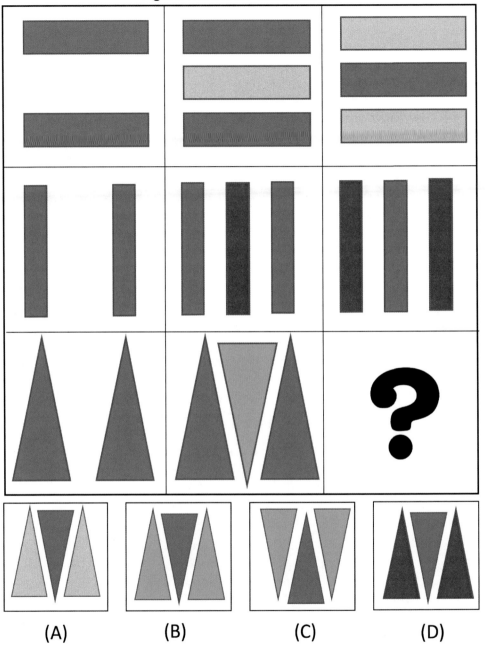

(A) (B) (C) (D)

Figure Matrices: Question 22

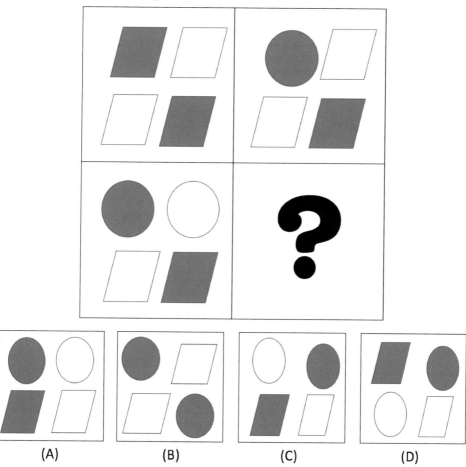

(A) (B) (C) (D)

Figure Matrices: Question 23

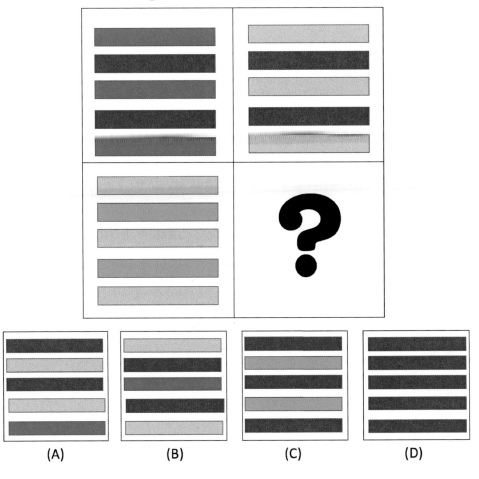

(A)   (B)   (C)   (D)

Figure Matrices: Question 24

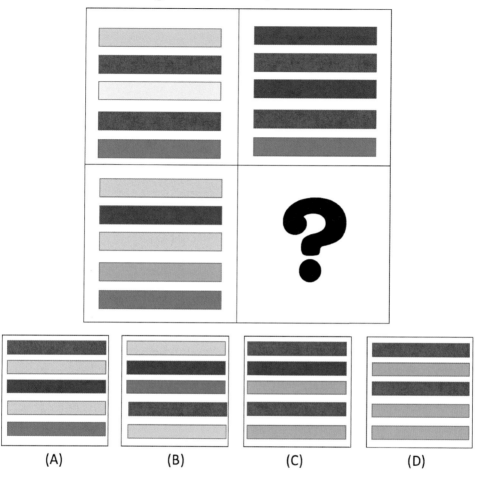

(A)   (B)   (C)   (D)

Figure Matrices: Question 25

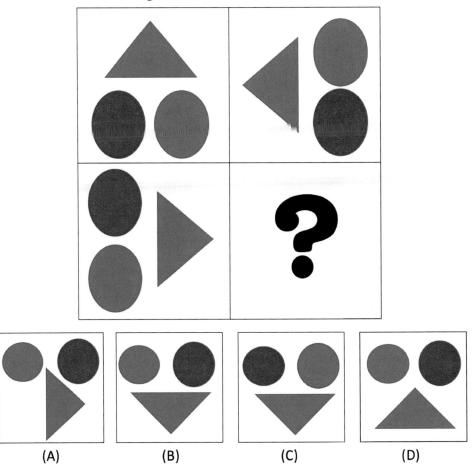

(A)   (B)   (C)   (D)

Figure Matrices: Answer Key

Question	Answer
1	B
2	A
3	D
4	B
5	D
6	B
7	A
8	B
9	D
10	C
11	D
12	D
13	D

Question	Answer
14	A
15	B
16	D
17	D
18	A
19	B
20	C
21	B
22	B
23	C
24	A
25	B

Please See Appendix B for a detailed explanation for each of these answers. Appendix B is written for adults to explain to children how a piece of critical thinking occurred on a problem. Tip: use this review time as a discussion platform on other ways the child may have found the answers. Note: Questions 20-25 were from a different (but similar) Gifted and Talented Test Trainer; congratulations if you answered all of them correctly!

Visual Analysis: Paper Folding

Paper folding is a practice of visualizing symmetry. Each question shows a piece of paper that is folded and cut. The answers all show what the paper will look like when it is unfolded. You can make a quick demonstration of this by folding a piece of paper in half, cutting a half heart shape out and then showing the student how it looks when unfolded.

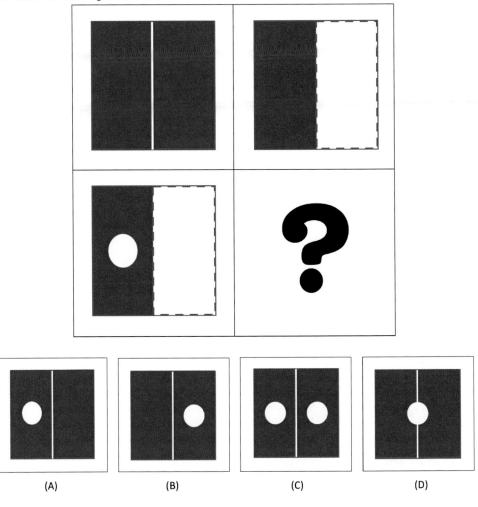

(A)   (B)   (C)   (D)

Let's do the first one together. Here the paper is folded in half along the white line, then a hole is punched. Which answer shows what the paper looks like unfolded? Answer C is correct; it shows two holes punched in the proper (symmetrical) locations.

Paper Folding: Question 1

(A)   (B)   (C)   (D)

Paper Folding: Question 2

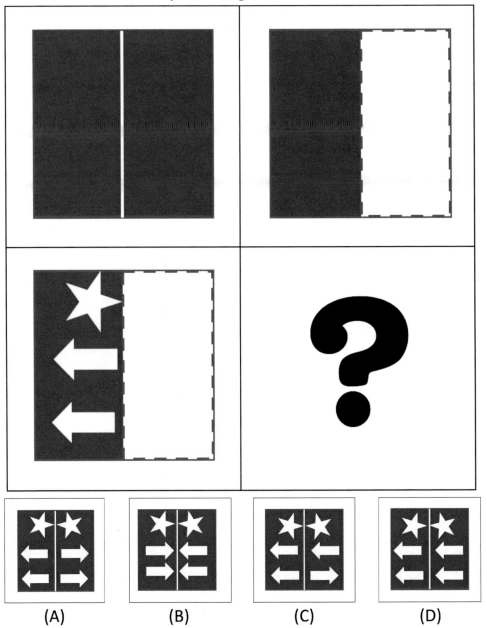

Paper Folding: Question 3

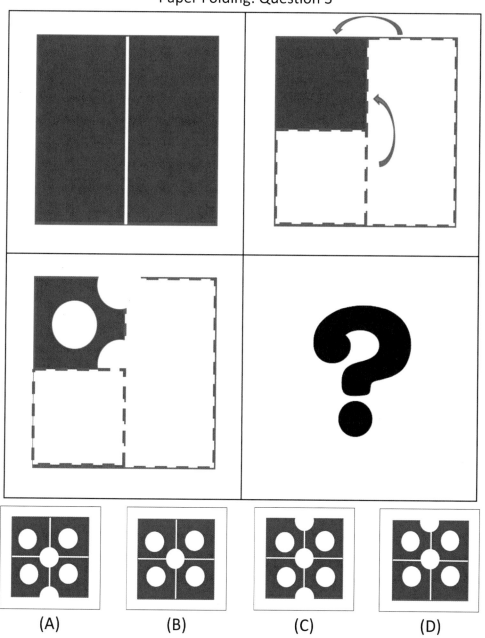

(A) (B) (C) (D)

(A) (B) (C) (D)

Paper Folding: Question 5

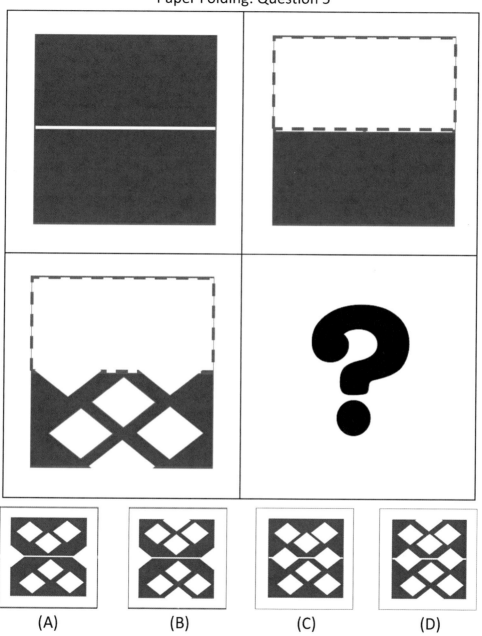

(A)   (B)   (C)   (D)

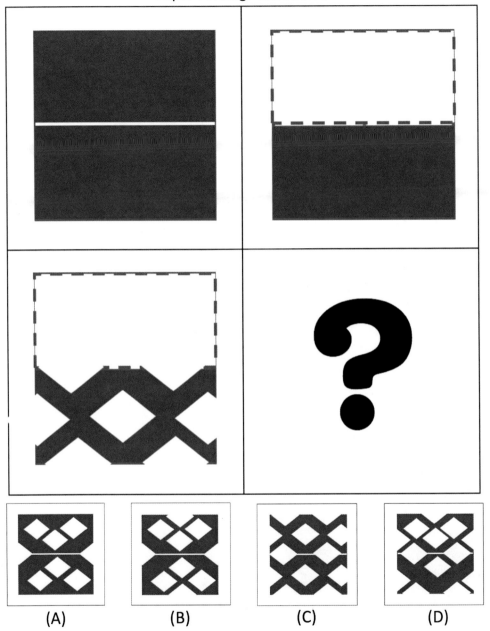

(A) (B) (C) (D)

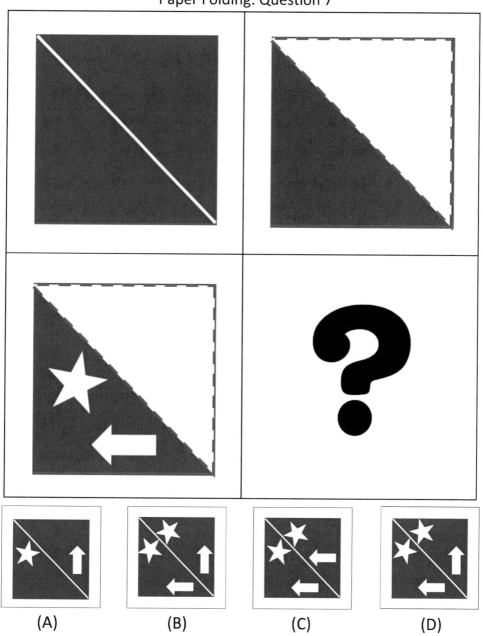

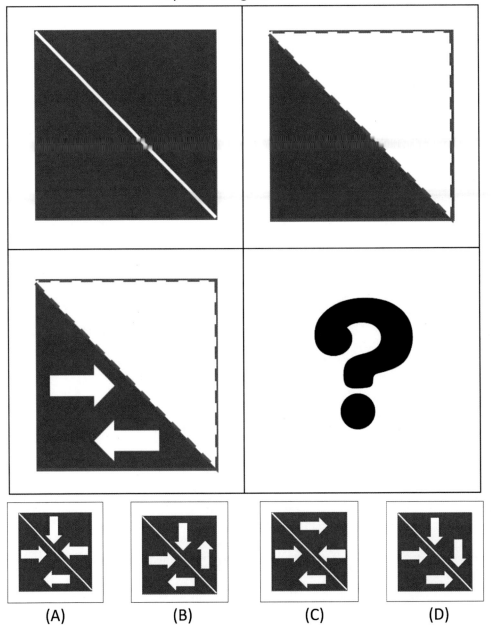

(A)   (B)   (C)   (D)

(A)   (B)   (C)   (D)

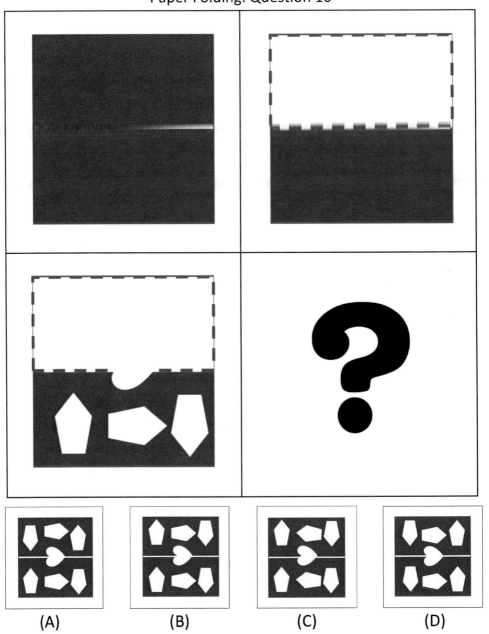

(A)　　　　(B)　　　　(C)　　　　(D)

(A)   (B)   (C)   (D)

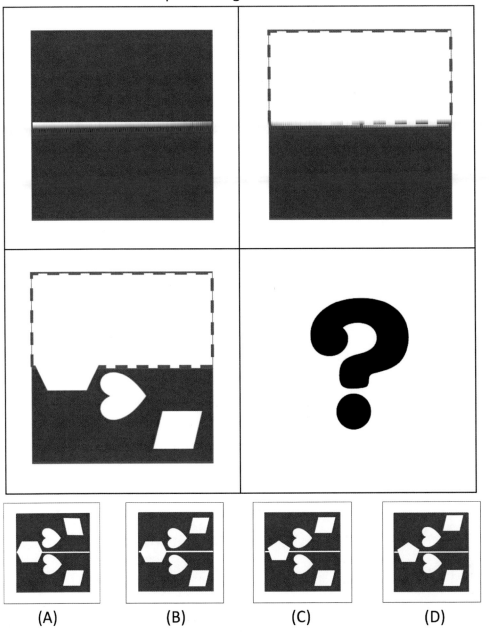

(A)   (B)   (C)   (D)

(A)   (B)   (C)   (D)

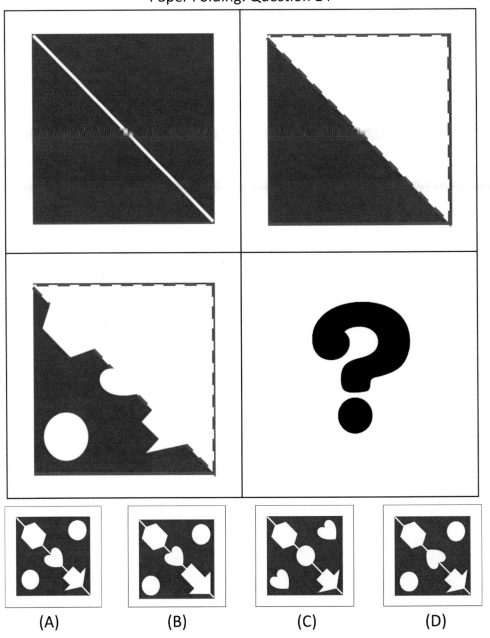

(A)   (B)   (C)   (D)

(A)   (B)   (C)   (D)

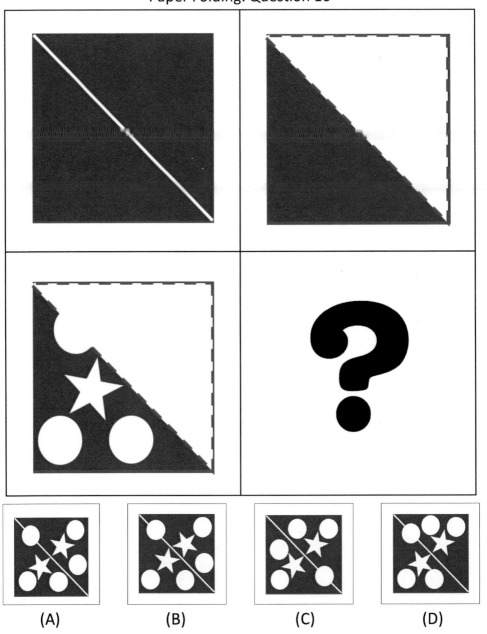

(A)　　　　(B)　　　　(C)　　　　(D)

Paper Folding: Answer Key

Question	Answer
1	C
2	A
3	C
4	B
5	D
6	C
7	D
8	B
9	D
10	A
11	C
12	A
13	D
14	A
15	C
16	B

Please See Appendix C for a detailed explanation for each of these answers. Appendix C is written for adults to explain to children how a piece of critical thinking occurred on a problem. Tip: use this review time as a discussion platform on other ways the child may have found the answers.

Numeric Skills

Numeric Skills: Number Series

Each of these number series show a particular pattern. Pick the number that is the next number in the series. Tip: patterns may be made by adding, subtracting, multiplying or dividing by a certain number.

1.   480   240   120   60   30   ?

   a) 50   b) 15   c) 45   d) 23   e) 24

2.   512   256   128   64   32   ?

   a) 16   b) 26   c) 33   d) 24   e) 34

3.   17   13   11   7   ?

   a) 2   b) 9   c) 1   d) 11   e) 5

4.   448   224   112   56   28   ?

   a) 27   b) 14   c) 21   d) 35   e) 42

5.   18   19   38   76   ?

   a) 140   b) 340   c) 252   d) 152   e) 146

6.   **1**   **3**   **6**   **10**   **15**   **21**   **?**

a) 28   b) 26   c) 25   d) 24   e) 29

7.   **1**   **5**   **10**   **20**   **40**   **?**

a) 50   b) 80   c) 60   d) 100   e) 65

8.   **2**   **3**   **5**   **7**   **11**   **13**   **?**

a) 21   b) 24   c) 13   d) 33   e) 17

9.   **8**   **16**   **32**   **64**   **?**

a) 65   b) 123   c) 128   d) 132   e) 256

10.   **5**   **10**   **20**   **40**   **80**   **?**

a) 140   b) 120   c) 180   d) 160   e) 240

11.   **80**   **40**   **20**   **10**   **?**

a) 10   b) 5   c) 15   d) 2   e) 0

12.   **12**   **23**   **34**   **45**   **56**   **?**

a) 85   b) 57   c) 76   d) 78   e) 67

13.   **102**   **020**   **203**   **030**   **304**   **?**

a) 050   b) 040   c) 405   d) 40   e) 004

14. <u>1   3   6   10   15   ?</u>

a) 20   b) 18   c) 21   d) 29   e) 31

15. <u>111   212   313   ?</u>

a) 141   b) 414   c) 151   d) 413   e) 314

16. <u>3X1   X13   13X   3X1   ?</u>

a) X13   b) X31   c) Y13   d) 31   e) 13

17. <u>10   15   30   60   120   ?</u>

a) 450   b) 340   c) 220   d) 210   e) 240

18. <u>1   4   2   5   3   ?</u>

a) 5   b) 6   c) 4   d) 7   e) 8

19. <u>15   20   40   80   160   ?</u>

a) 320   b) 550   c) 220   d) 430   e) 190

20 <u>8   13   18   23   28   ?</u>

a) 36   b) 34   c) 24   d) 33   e) 29

21. <u>61   52   43   34   ?</u>

a) 34   b) 24   c) 25   d) 33   e) 16

22. <u>2 3 5 8 13 ?</u>

   a) 21   b) 19   c) 15   d) 18   e) 24

23. <u>1 2 2 3 3 ?</u>

   a) 2   b) 4   c) 3   d) 5   e) 6

24. <u>5 4 6 5 7 ?</u>

   a) 4   b) 6   c) 5   d) 7   e) 8

25. <u>10 12 14 16 18 ?</u>

   a) 22   b) 25   c) 19   d) 20   e) 21

Think Critically

If there are 4 crows on a fence and a goblin throws a rock at one crow and knocks it off the fence, how many crows are there left on the fence?

Answer

There are no crows left on the fence. If one crow gets knocked off the fence the other three will be spooked and fly away.

Number Series: Answer Key

Question	Answer	Question	Answer
1	B	14	C
2	A	15	B
3	E	16	A
4	B	17	E
5	D	18	B
6	A	19	A
7	B	20	D
8	E	21	C
9	C	22	A
10	D	23	C
11	B	24	B
12	E	25	D
13	B		

Please See Appendix D for a detailed explanation on how to find these answers and **additional practice**. Appendix D is written for adults to explain to children how a particular piece of critical thinking occurred on a problem. Tip: use this review time as a discussion platform on other ways the child may have found the answers.

Numeric Skills: Number Puzzles

Number Puzzles are a clever way to introduce the student to concepts found in algebra. Here we substitute numbers for shapes and the student must solve a simple math problem given a question with one or more shapes, a math operator (addition or subtraction) and a number that the shape represents. *Tip: when you see two or more of the same shape that means to add the number value of those shapes together. For example, if a square is equal to one, two squares next to each other are equal to two.*

1. 6 X ▣ = (?) | ▣ = 9

    a) 46   b) 54   c) 63   d) 56   e) 52

2. 72 / ▲ = (?) | ▲ = 8

    a) 9   b) 7   c) 11   d) 8   e) 6

3. ◆ X 6 = (?) | ◆ = 12 / 4

    a) 15   b) 24   c) 12   d) 18   e) 24

4. 72 + ⬡⬡ = (?) | ⬡ = 7 + 2

    a) 81   b) 90   c) 86   d) 76   e) 92

5. 37 - ✕ = (?) | ✕ = 7 x 2

    a) 35   b) 51   c) 28   d) 30   e) 23

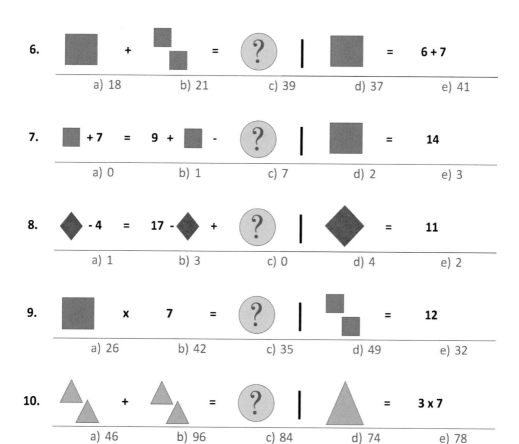

6. ◼ + ◪ = ? | ◼ = 6 + 7

    a) 18   b) 21   c) 39   d) 37   e) 41

7. ◼ + 7 = 9 + ◼ - ? | ◼ = 14

    a) 0   b) 1   c) 7   d) 2   e) 3

8. ◆ - 4 = 17 - ◆ + ? | ◆ = 11

    a) 1   b) 3   c) 0   d) 4   e) 2

9. ◼ x 7 = ? | ◪ = 12

    a) 26   b) 42   c) 35   d) 49   e) 32

10. ▲▲ + ▲▲ = ? | ▲ = 3 x 7

    a) 46   b) 96   c) 84   d) 74   e) 78

Think Critically
Can you count from 9 to 1 backwards?
(Answer on Next Page)

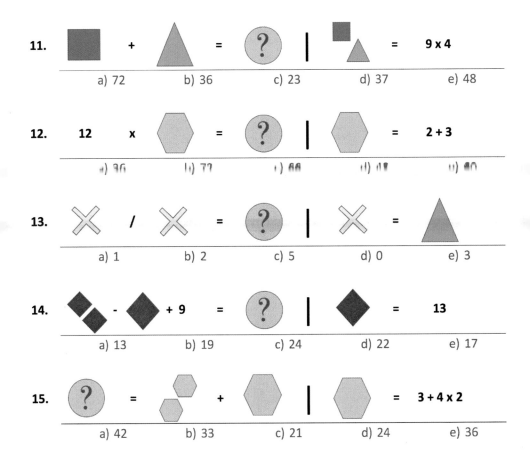

11. ⬛ + 🔺 = (?) | ⬛🔺 = 9 x 4

      a) 72   b) 36   c) 23   d) 37   e) 48

12. 12 x ⬡ = (?) | ⬡ = 2 + 3

      a) 36   b) 72   c) 68   d) 18   e) 80

13. ✕ / ✕ = (?) | ✕ = 🔺

      a) 1   b) 2   c) 5   d) 0   e) 3

14. ◆◆ - ◆ + 9 = (?) | ◆ = 13

      a) 13   b) 19   c) 24   d) 22   e) 17

15. (?) = ⬡⬡ + ⬡ | ⬡ = 3 + 4 x 2

      a) 42   b) 33   c) 21   d) 24   e) 36

Answer
1 2 3 4 5 6 7 8 9
Break the question into 2 parts.
"Can you count from 9 to 1 backwards?"
Part 1: Count from 9 to 1 (9 8 7 6 5 4 3 2 1...)
Part 2: do it backwards (1 2 3 4 5 6 7 8 9)

Number Puzzles: Answer Key

Question	Answer
1	B
2	A
3	D
4	B
5	E
6	C
7	D
8	A
9	B
10	C
11	B
12	E
13	A
14	D
15	B

Please See Appendix E for a detailed explanation for how to find each of these answers. Appendix E is written for adults to explain to children how a piece of critical thinking occurred on a problem. Tip: use this review time as a discussion platform on other ways the child may have found the answers.

Numeric Skills: Number Analogies

1.

$$26 > 13$$

$$42 > 21$$

$$30 > \; ?$$

20	15	10	30	25
A	B	C	D	E

2.

6 > 19

4 > 17

8 > ?

24	32	27	23	21
A	B	C	D	E

3.

$$7 > 21$$

$$15 > 45$$

$$11 > \;?$$

A	B	C	D	E
36	28	33	41	30

4.

| 2 | > | 18 |

| 4 | > | 36 |

| 6 | > | ? |

| 50 | 31 | 62 | 54 | 35 |
| A | B | C | D | E |

5.

9	>	26

4	>	21

20	>	?

25	37	34	50	44
A	B	C	D	E

6.

| 24 | > | 6 |

| 36 | > | 9 |

| 16 | > | ? |

| 4 | 5 | 9 | 8 | 10 |
| A | B | C | D | E |

7.

30 > 21

10 > 1

19 > ?

A. 5
B. 10
C. 14
D. 7
E. 16

8.

| 2 | > | 22 |

| 4 | > | 44 |

| 3 | > | ? |

| 26 | 40 | 29 | 30 | 33 |
| A | B | C | D | E |

9.

$4 > 24$

$2 > 22$

$3 > ?$

A	B	C	D	E
24	19	21	23	20

10.

| 3 | > | 25 |

| 8 | > | 30 |

| 1 | > | ? |

| 21 | 26 | 23 | 29 | 22 |
| A | B | C | D | E |

11.

$$20 > 10$$

$$46 > 23$$

$$90 > \text{?}$$

10	36	40	45	50
A	B	C	D	E

12.

| 5 | > | 35 |

| 9 | > | 63 |

| 3 | > | ? |

| 18 | 33 | 24 | 21 | 27 |
| A | B | C | D | E |

13.

$$17 > 14$$

$$21 > 18$$

$$14 > \;?$$

34	27	24	13	11
A	B	C	D	E

14.

30 > 90

15 > 45

20 > ?

30	80	60	40	50
A	B	C	D	E

15.

| 12 | > | 3 |

| 38 | > | 29 |

| 24 | > | ? |

| 15 | 13 | 17 | 16 | 18 |
| A | B | C | D | E |

16.

| 9 | > | 3 |

| 21 | > | 7 |

| 30 | > | ? |

| 22 | 11 | 10 | 14 | 21 |
| A | B | C | D | E |

17.

6 > 29

5 > 28

3 > ?

A. 23 B. 27 C. 28 D. 21 E. 26

18.

$$18 > 9$$

$$14 > 7$$

$$22 > \; ?$$

A	B	C	D	E
11	7	8	15	9

19.

| 9 | > | 36 |

| 3 | > | 12 |

| 10 | > | ? |

| 36 | 22 | 37 | 34 | 40 |
| A | B | C | D | E |

20.

13 > 29

10 > 26

9 > ?

A	B	C	D	E
30	23	25	21	18

Number Analogies: Answer Key

Question	Answer
1	B
2	E
3	C
4	D
5	B
6	A
7	B
8	E
9	D
10	C

Question	Answer
11	D
12	D
13	E
14	C
15	A
16	C
17	E
18	A
19	E
20	C

There is no detailed explanation for this section. You should simply review the questions missed by the student. Tip: In this section there are only four possible patterns. Something is added to each number, something is subtracted from each number, the number is doubling or the number is being cut in half.

Language Skills

Language Skills: Sentence Completion

This section is a standard fill in the blank type of response. Read the question and look for clues as to what the right word is. This isn't a test of how large your vocabulary is; it is more about the finding a clue and making an educated guess of the answer.

1. **After many hours the girl became _____ with the sword and the pen. She was able to slice fruit and compose essays with ease.**
   a) dirt　　　b) prosperous　c) plausible　　d) enlightened　e) proficient

2. **The plan was put to a vote, and after voting the decision was _____.**
   a) blundered　b) unanimous　c) ingenious　　d) recount　　e) controversy

3. **No tool was available, so Robert had to create a _____ hammer.**
   a) vital　　　b) context　　c) makeshift　　d) distinct　　e) monotonous

4. **Trying to redirect an argument by attacking the reputation of the opponent is a(n) _____ and does not prove the position as right or wrong.**
   a) point　　　b) fallacy　　c) riposte　　　d) falsey　　e) herring

5. **After the TNT was dropped into the mine shaft and detonated, all that remained was _____, fragmented wood and broken equipment.**
   a) defect　　b) rubble　　c) wheel　　　d) blast　　e) tract

6. After a government collapses the result is _____ and civil disorder. All services stop and no one is in charge.

   a) anarchy   b) antimony   c) revolution   d) dictatorship   e) church

7. He was nervous about how big the crowd was, but he managed to maintain his _____ through his speech.

   a) innovation   b) beacon   c) pursue   d) futile   e) composure

8. In response to rebel attacks within the border government decided to place a(n) _____ on all firearms imported to the island to stop the trade of weapons.

   a) trade deal   b) embargo   c) levy   d) ball   e) tax

9. The attorney was already conducting a _____ investigation.

   a) ample   b) preliminary   c) former   d) parody   e) equivalent

10. The bacteria can be very dangerous so antibiotics must be taken at the _____ of symptoms.

    a) painstaking   b) burden   c) chronological d) provoke   e) onset

Think Critically

A man is on a trip with a fox, goose, and a sack of corn. He comes upon a stream, which he has to cross, and finds a tiny boat which he can use. The problem is that he can only take himself and either the fox, goose, or the corn across at a time. It is not possible for him to leave the fox alone with the goose (the fox will eat the goose), or the goose alone with the corn (the goose will eat the corn). How can he get all safely over the stream?

11. The friar demanded that the weary group of travelers _____ their traditions in favor of the new religion.

a) renounce   b) exemplify   c) evolve   d) hang   e) facilitate

12. The mosquito net was _____ with many holes to allow for air to circulate while tight enough to restrict flying insects.

a) flair   b) porous   c) balmy   d) metal   e) bountiful

13. She was a great senator; everyone held her in high _____.

a) primitive   b) apparel   c) esteem   d) economy   e) subjective

14. Before the ship was retired to the boneyard, a celebration was held to _____ its long life of service to the empire.

a) fortify   b) shovel   c) banter   d) decree   e) commemorate

15. After the factory closed down, most of the people living there lived in _____.

a) predicament   b) evolved   c) subsequent   d) poverty   e) stationary

Answer

The man will take the goose over first and come back. Then he will take the fox, and bring the goose back from the other side. On his next trip, he will take the corn and come back alone to get the goose. Finally, he will take the goose over completing the mission to cross the stream.

16. The first visit to the Space Station is said to cause a(n) _____ attitude in all travelers leaving them with feelings of awe and inspiration.

    a) coded   b) sublime   c) satisfied   d) arrogant   e) subliminal

17. Railroads used to be a(n) _____ business. In their height, railroads made many people in the western world a great many fortunes.

    a) bizarre   b) lucrative   c) chair   d) voracious   e) luminous

18. It wasn't _____ to run in the halls so I walked like normal.

    a) poor   b) rule   c) appropriate   d) sad   e) great

19. A Soldier will shine her boots and polish the buttons on her dress uniform to _____ pride, duty and discipline in herself and her unit.

    a) instill   b) knife   c) install   d) shackle   e) reject

20. The new smartphone was being hailed as a technological _____ .

    a) dominate   b) cumulative   c) marvel   d) tangible   e) vow

End Of Section!
Keep Up The Good Work!

Sentence Completion: Answer Key

Question	Answer	Question	Answer
1	E	11	A
2	B	12	B
3	C	13	C
4	B	14	E
5	B	15	D
6	A	16	B
7	E	17	B
8	B	18	C
9	B	19	A
10	E	20	C

There is no detailed explanation for this section. Review the questions missed with the test taker. Tips:

- Review each answer in a question and try to force yourself to pick from the top two answers. This will help make sure you have considered each question thoroughly.
- The elimination method works for this section just as you did for the visual problems in previous sections.
- As with all language sections, having a strong vocabulary is key to winning.

Language Skills: Verbal Classification

Questions in this section will show you three words that are related in a certain way. Pick a word from the set of answers that are also related in that same certain way. To say it another way, you will be classifying the words. For example, they could be items in a kitchen, things that you do or types of food. When you figure out the classification, choose a word from the answers that most closely fits that classification.

1.   **disfavor**   **depricate**   **detract**   _____
     a) compliment   b) discount   c) approve
     d) upvote   e) endorse

2.   **bike**   **scooter**   **skateboard**   _____
     a) car   b) skate   c) walk
     d) jog   e) ride

3.   **orange**   **mango**   **pineapple**   _____
     a) beat   b) apple   c) potato
     d) lime   e) tomato

4.   **desert**   **mountain**   **swamp**   _____
     a) terrain   b) farming   c) house
     d) grass   e) oasis

5.   **antagonist**   **minor**   **major**   _____
     a) play   b) novel   c) nonfiction
     d) protagonist   e) opera

6. **jet**   **car**   **tank**   _____
   a) skateboard   b) scooter   c) tractor
   d) sailboat   e) motorcycle

7. **heart**   **liver**   **brain**   _____
   a) bone   b) skin   c) eye
   d) hair   e) stomach

8. **blackberry**   **strawberry**   **blueberry**   _____
   a) apple   b) cherry   c) pineapple
   d) raspberry   e) yogurt

9. **preschool**   **elementary school**   **high school**   _____
   a) test   b) homework   c) education
   d) university   e) books

10. **worry**   **anger**   **fear**   _____
    a) sadness   b) joy   c) arrogant
    d) alpha   e) estatic

11. **earth** **mars** **jupiter** _____

    a) enterprise   b) mountain   c) galaxy

    d) circle   e) space

12. **arctic** **subarctic** **humid** _____

    a) country   b) state   c) tropical

    d) planet   e) nation

13. **camera** **lighting** **sound**

    a) actors   b) director   c) producer

    d) special effects   e) makeup artist

14. **spoon** **tank** **apple** _____

    a) catch   b) phone   c) science

    d) math   e) philosophy

15. **respectful** **polite** **well behaved** _____

    a) antagonist   b) exult   c) courteous

    d) impressive   e) excavate

16. **breastplate**   **helmet**   **gauntlet**   _____
   a) shield   b) head   c) arm
   d) gigantic   e) hand

17. **up**   **down**   **beside**   _____
   a) navigate   b) around   c) map
   d) direct   e) instruction

18. **speak**   **sing**   **shout**   _____
   a) taxi   b) jam   c) snake
   d) coil   e) jog

19. **monarchy**   **republic**   **dictatorship**   _____
   a) continental   b) geography   c) national
   d) democracy   e) government

20. **table**   **diving board**   **runway**   _____
   a) floor   b) keyboard   c) hillside
   d) boat   e) mouse

Think Critically

An old wooden sail ship called "Athens" takes a voyage around the world. As the ship sails around to each port the sailors must make repairs. One by one each piece of the ship is replaced for a newer part. 20 years later the ship has returned to its home with every piece of the ship replaced. Is it the same ship?

21. **pistol**   **rifle**   **bow**   _____
    a) spear   b) bullet   c) axe
    d) sling   e) shield

22. **librarian**   **teacher**   **instructor**   _____
    a) luxury   b) hamlet   c) library
    d) historian   e) school

23. **finger**   **claw**   **hoof**   _____
    a) animal   b) nose   c) horse
    d) talon   e) vulture

24. **aroma**   **odor**   **stench**   _____
    a) fumes   b) escalate   c) assume
    d) sparse   e) dependent

25. **reading**   **math**   **science**   _____
    a) bored   b) writing   c) old
    d) teacher   e) school

Answer

There is no right answer! This is a philosophy question called a paradox. If you said it was a new ship now ask yourself exactly when did the ship become 'a new ship'. Was it when the first repair was made? Or was it when the very last piece of the ship was replaced? If you said it is still the same ship, how can you say that if every part of the old ship was replaced?

Verbal Classification: Answer Key

Question	Answer	Question	Answer
1	B	14	B
2	B	15	C
3	D	16	A
4	E	17	B
5	D	18	E
6	C	19	D
7	E	20	A
8	D	21	D
9	D	22	D
10	A	23	D
11	D	24	A
12	C	25	B
13	D		

There is no appendix for Verbal Classification explaining the correct answers. Review the answer sheet here and have a discussion on which questions were missed and what the correct answer is. **Some of these are intentionally hard!** Tips for some of the tricky questions:

- Question 1: The category is "words that begin with D"
- Question 11: The category is "things that are round"
- Question 14: The category is "things you can touch"
- Question 20: The category is "things that have a flat surface"

Language Skills: Verbal Analogies

This section has the familiar, "this word" is to "that word" as "other word" is to "[pick a word]". The only difference is the related words are separated by a |----------| instead of linking with the 'is to' 'as' words as you have probably seen before. So look at the first two words presented, figure out their relation, then look at the next word and pick a word from the answer set that has that same relation.

1.   **innocent |----------| guilty**
          pessimist |----------| _____
   a) painstaking   b) unhappy   c) optimist
   d) hostile   e) encounter

2.   **famous |----------| unknown**
          miniature |----------| _____
   a) tiny   b) well known   c) prejudice
   d) extract   e) massive

3.   **join |----------| separate**
          foreign |----------| _____
   a) international   b) tangible   c) domestic
   d) drastic   e) retaliate

4.   **hunger |----------| thirst**
          skilled |----------| _____
   a) prominent   b) inept   c) intelligent
   d) talented   e) commend

5.   **body |----------| arm**
          nation |----------| _____
   a) guest   b) swarm   c) capital
   d) boycott   e) world

6.   **country** |----------| **rural**
        city |----------| _____

a) vibrant   b) lure   c) pasture
d) remote   e) urban

7.   **fast** |----------| **slow**
     current |----------| __

a) clvlc   b) modern   c) reinforce
d) hoax   e) former

8.   **neat** |----------| **clean**
     ancient |----------| _____

a) provoke   b) primitive   c) awe
d) modern   e) beacon

9.   **dish** |----------| **dish soap**
     hand |----------| _____

a) car soap   b) liquid soap   c) hand soap
d) bar soap   e) laundry soap

10. **key** |----------| **piano**
     second |----------| _____

a) vibrant   b) knack   c) minute
d) third   e) clock

11.   **scrutinize** |----------| **inspect**
        disagree |----------| _____

a) marvel   b) dialogue   c) dissent
d) soothe   e) agree

12.   **expensive** |----------| **cheap**
        figurative |----------| _____

a) terminate   b) literal   c) unanimous
d) imaginary   e) lure

13.   **fake** |----------| **counterfeit**
           move |----------| _____

a) apprehensive   b) propel   c) boisterous
d) predicament   e) stop

14.   **fail** |----------| **succeed**
        remain |----------| _____

a) swarm   b) linger   c) vacate
d) possess   e) cordial

15.   **chill** |----------| **freeze**
           heat |----------| _____

a) dominate   b) stove   c) temperature
d) candle   e) ignite

16. calm |----------| peaceful
   detest |----------| _____
   a) loathe   b) cultivate   c) cordial
   d) supplement   e) admire

17 scared |----------| frightened
   free |----------| _____
   a) colide   b) salvage   c) enslave
   d) liberate   e) restain

18. idle |----------| inactive
   evade |----------| _____
   a) ample   b) capture   c) elude
   d) control   e) objective

19. make |----------| destroy
   safe |----------| _____
   a) confident   b) unique   c) treacherous
   d) designate   e) easy

20. leader |----------| follower
   uncertain |----------| _____
   a) prosper   b) remorse   c) commend
   d) unlikely   e) inevitable

21. wrong |----------| incorrect
unenthusiastic |----------| _____
- a) context
- b) ingenious
- c) reluctant
- d) excited
- e) rigorous

22. hurt |----------| harm
fall |----------| _____
- a) economy
- b) plummet
- c) onset
- d) fly
- e) adhere

23. explain |----------| clarify
barrier |----------| _____
- a) obstacle
- b) eerie
- c) guest
- d) genre
- e) adapt

24. minuscule |----------| small
big |----------| _____
- a) hostile
- b) trait
- c) tiny
- d) massive
- e) remorse

End Of Section!
Keep Up The Good Work!

Verbal Analogies: Answer Key

Question	Answer	Question	Answer
1	C	13	B
2	E	14	C
3	C	15	E
4	D	16	A
5	C	17	D
6	E	18	C
7	E	19	C
8	B	20	E
9	C	21	C
10	C	22	B
11	C	23	A
12	B	24	D

There is no appendix for Verbal Analogies explaining the correct answers. Review the answer sheet here and have a discussion on which questions were missed and what the correct answer is.

Tips for the test:
- The first word pairs are RELATED in one of three types
  - Word A is similar to Word B (such as miniscule |-| small)
  - Word A is opposite to Word B (such as make |-| destroy)
  - Word A is a part of Word B (such as key |-| piano)

First find the RELATION then use elimination method to find that same RELATION.

Appendix A: Figure Classification Answer Guide

Here we explain each question and answer found in the Figure Classification quiz. The answer is found in the text under the question.

Figure Classification: Question 1

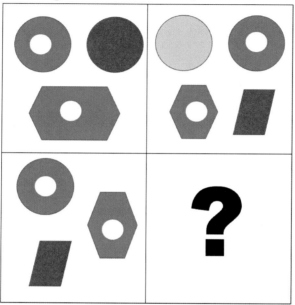

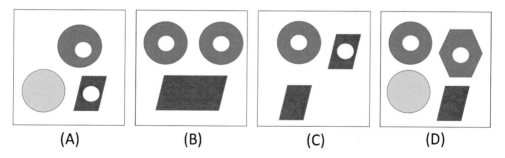

(A)   (B)   (C)   (D)

What is the same about all of these pictures? All of the squares have a circle with a dot in the middle, and a hexagon with a dot in the middle. The correct answer is D.

Figure Classification: Question 2

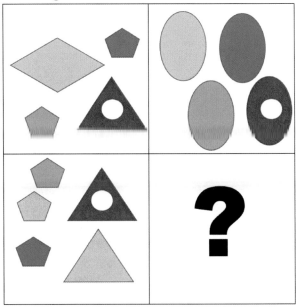

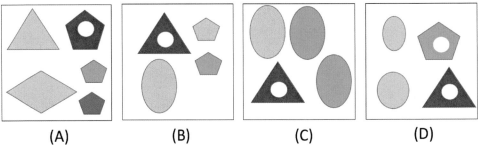

(A)   (B)   (C)   (D)

There are a lot of different items in these squares, but the thing that is the same here are the colors. Every square has at least one red, green, yellow, and blue item. The only answer that has one item of each color is answer A, so it is correct.

Figure Classification: Question 3

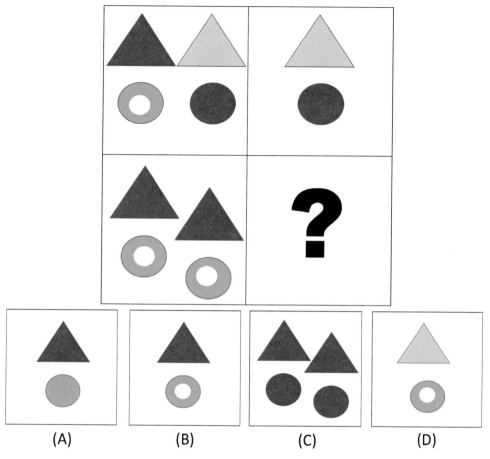

(A)   (B)   (C)   (D)

For this question we will have to use process of elimination, because there isn't a clear pattern in every square. When you look at the possible answers, C sticks out as the most different because it is all red, so let's eliminate that one. The remaining three are all triangles and a circle. We should eliminate D next, because in the squares provided we never have only yellow and green in an example. Between A and B do we pick the one with the dot or the one without? We should pick the dot because in our examples, 2 of the squares have a green circle with a dot. B is the best answer.

Figure Classification: Question 4

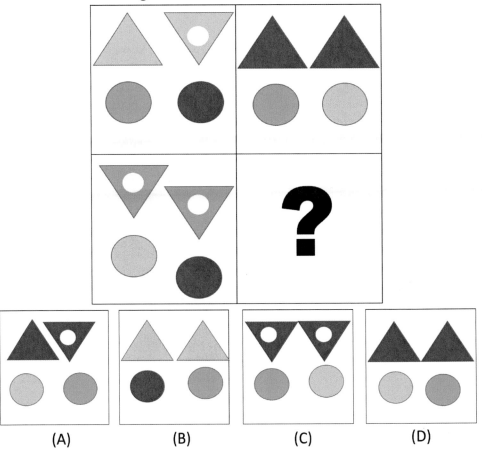

(A) (B) (C) (D)

The answer is D. Can you figure out why? The top right example picture has two red triangles, a green circle and a yellow circle. Answer D has this same set of shapes in these same colors. It's the safest bet on a right answer. Answer B looks like the top left picture but one of the triangles is missing a white circle. Answers A and C also look like the top right picture but they have extra white circles in the red triangles.

Figure Classification: Question 5

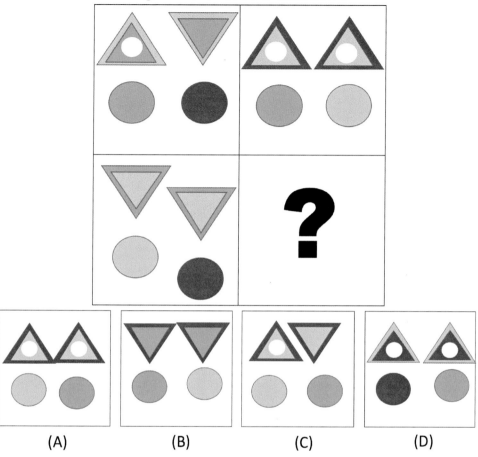

(A)　　　　　(B)　　　　　(C)　　　　　(D)

This question is the same idea as in question 4 except we have some more colors to look at. Answer A resembles the top right square MORE THAN any other answer resembles any of the example pictures.

Figure Classification: Question 6

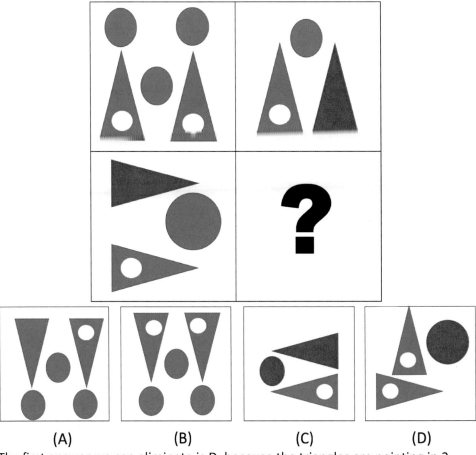

(A)	(B)	(C)	(D)

The first answer we can eliminate is D, because the triangles are pointing in 2 different directions. Of the remaining answers, B matches the best. A looks like the first square, but has 1 less dot, and C looks like the 3rd square but has a red circle instead of a blue circle. B is the best answer.

Figure Classification: Question 7

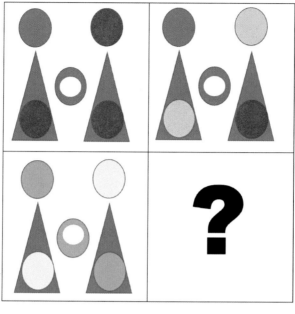

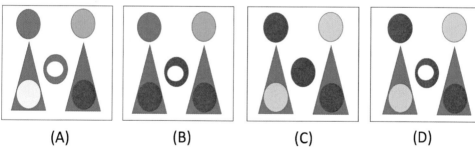

| (A) | (B) | (C) | (D) |

The answer here is D. This one was meant to be very hard so don't feel bad if you missed it. The middle circle is the key shape. The color of the middle circle in each sample is the same color as the top left circle in the picture (Eliminate answer B). Each middle circle also has a white circle in it (eliminate Answer C). Now which is more correct from answer A or D? Answer A has 4 different colors of circles, each sample only has 2 or 3 different colors of circles. Answer D is the winner.

Figure Classification: Question 8

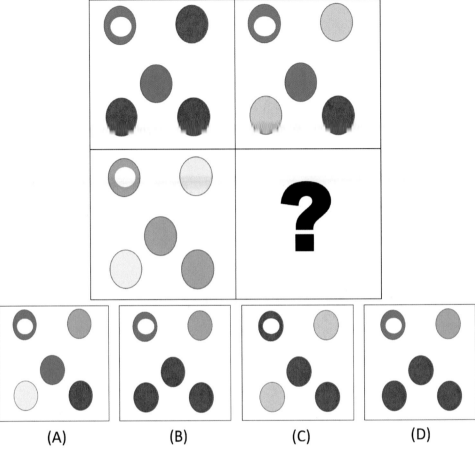

(A)　　　　(B)　　　　(C)　　　　(D)

Once again, we should eliminate answers that don't match well. A has too many colors so we should eliminate it. B and D have the same color on the bottom 3 circles, so we should be able to eliminate them. If we compare C to the squares, we can see that it has the same color scheme as the 3rd square, only swapping green with red and yellow with orange. C is the best answer.

Figure Classification: Question 9

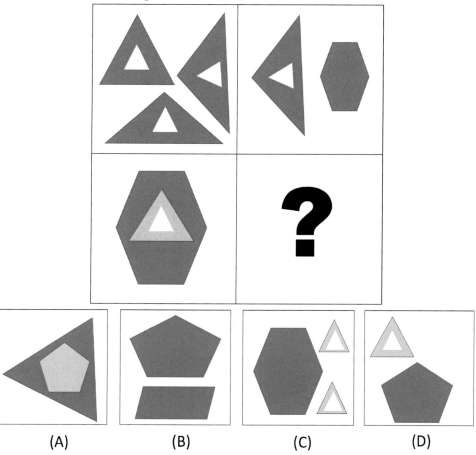

(A)   (B)   (C)   (D)

Answer C is the best pick here. Answers A, B and D all have a pentagon in them and this shape is nowhere to be seen in the example pictures.

Figure Classification: Question 10

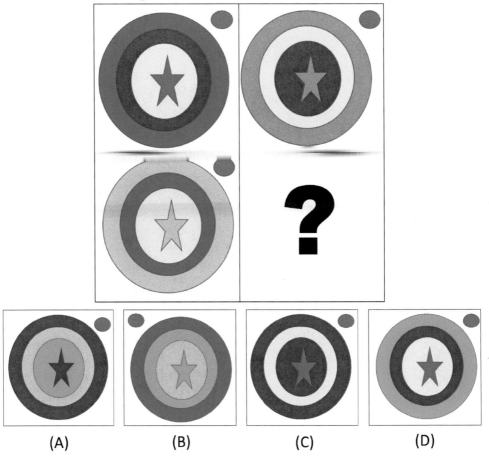

(A)   (B)   (C)   (D)

The Answer is A. In each picture the center star is the same color as the outer circle. Answer A has a red star and a red outer ring. The other answers do not follow this pattern.

Figure Classification: Question 11

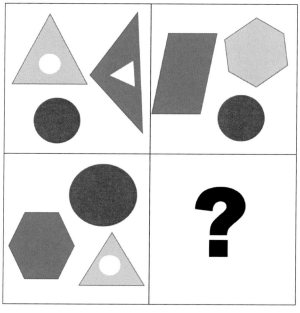

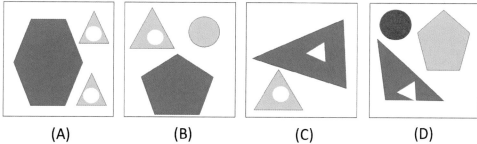

(A)   (B)   (C)   (D)

All answers shown here are missing a red circle except for Answer D. All sample pictures have similar shapes but each of them definitely has a red circle. This is part of the classification.

Figure Classification: Question 12

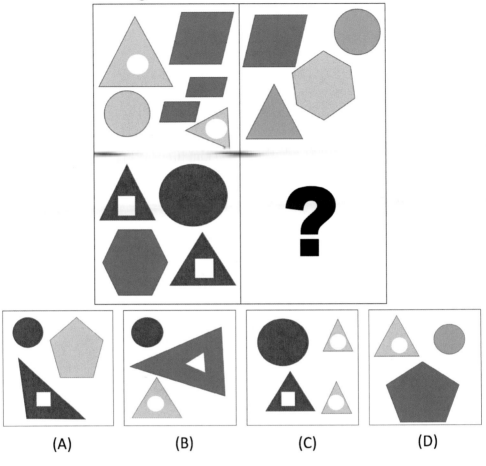

(A) (B) (C) (D)

The answer is A. Can you figure out why? Notice in each sample picture that the circle's color always matches the triangle's color. Answer A is the only one that does this. Don't be confused that B and C have two different colors of triangles, this does not match the pattern in the sample pictures. Notice how the top left and bottom left pictures have triangles of the same color.

Figure Classification: Question 13

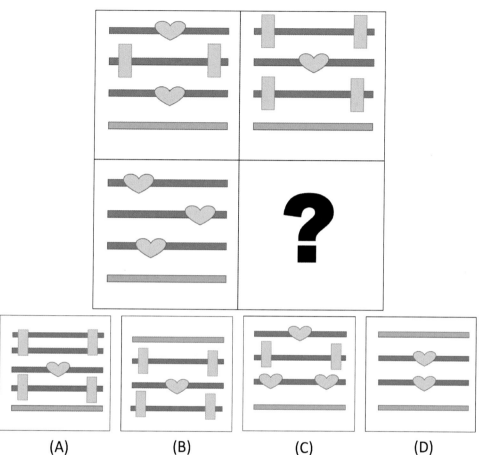

(A) (B) (C) (D)

In this question the shapes are just a distraction; what will help you find the answer is the colors. All of the squares have 3 blue lines on top and a green line on the bottom. The only answer that matches is C.

Figure Classification: Question 14

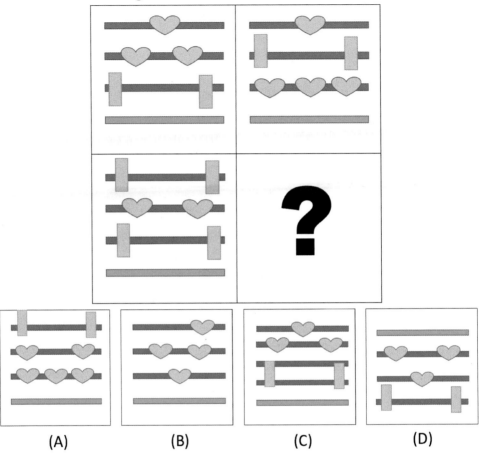

(A) (B) (C) (D)

We can start by looking at the lines like we did in the last question; A and B fit the pattern of 3 blue lines and a green line. Next we look at the shapes. B only has hearts while A has hearts and squares like in all of the squares, so A is the best answer.

Figure Classification: Question 15

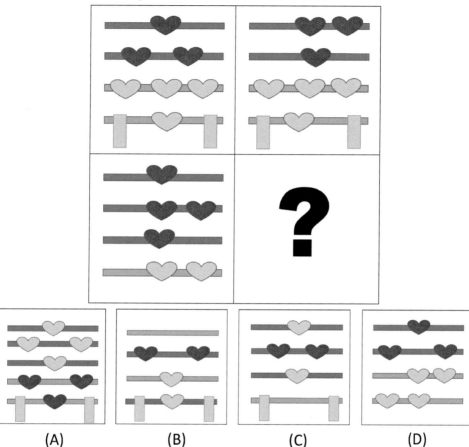

Let's look at the lines one more time – we can definitely eliminate A because it has too many. We can also probably eliminate B because the colors are in a different pattern than any of the squares. How can we pick between C and D? D is the best answer due to the arrangement of colors. In all of the squares, all of the red objects are above the yellow objects, so D is the better answer.

Figure Classification: Question 16

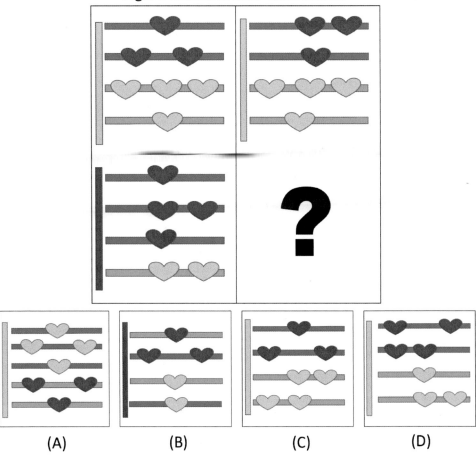

(A)   (B)   (C)   (D)

We can once again eliminate two answers because of the lines. A has too many, and B has the green lines in a different pattern. That leaves us with C and D. These two are very similar, so we just have to figure out which one is a little bit better answer. C seems a little bit better based on the number of hearts. In our example squares, we have 3 and 4 red hearts, just like C and D. We also have 2 or 4 yellow hearts, but no examples with only 3. So C is the slightly better answer.

Figure Classification: Question 17

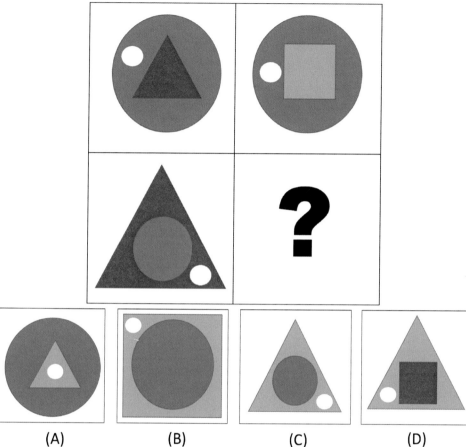

(A)   (B)   (C)   (D)

What is common among these 3 pictures? They all have a blue circle and a white dot. D doesn't have a blue circle, so we can eliminate it. A has a blue circle, but the triangle is green, and in the squares the 2 triangles are both red. A is eliminated. Between B and C, we should eliminate C because the triangle is green instead of red. B is correct because it has a blue circle and a green square.

Figure Classification: Question 18

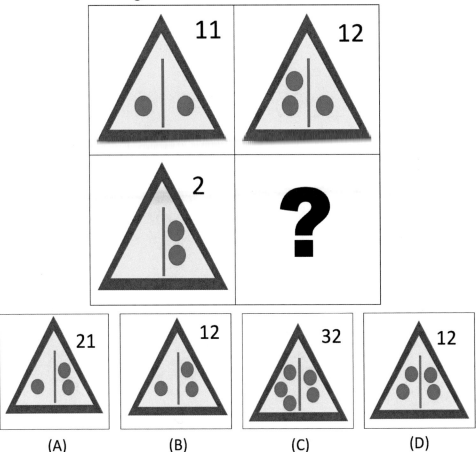

(A)   (B)   (C)   (D)

In this example we need to focus on the number and blue circles. The number gives us some information about which side of the line the blue circles should be on. In the first square we have 11 which is one circle on each side of the line. In the next square we have 12, with 1 circle on the right and 2 on the left. And the last square just has a 2, for 2 circles. Look at B – it also has 12 for the number and also has one circle on the left and 2 on the right. If we compare this to the 12 in our example square, we notice that they don't match. B is wrong because our example is showing us the first number is the number of circles on the right side, and the second number is the number of circles on the left. This means that A is correct because the number 2 means 2 on the right, and the 1 means 1 on the left. C is wrong because it should be 23 not 32.

Figure Classification: Question 19

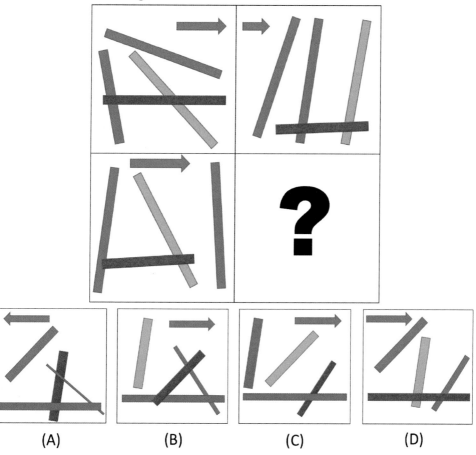

(A)　　　　(B)　　　　(C)　　　　(D)

The one thing that sticks out right away in the 3 squares is that there is a red line going from left to right in all of them. A, B, and C all have a blue line going from left to right which means that D is correct because it has a red line going horizontally.

Figure Classification: Question 20

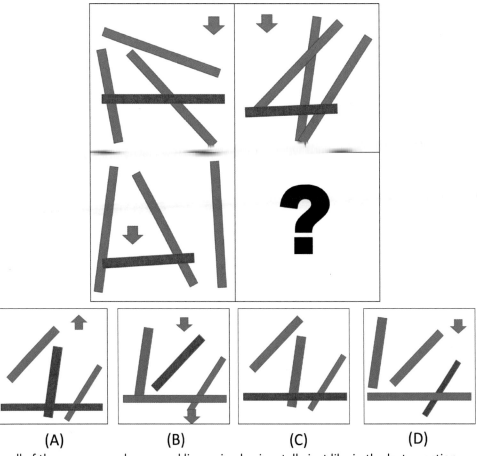

(A)   (B)   (C)   (D)

In all of the squares we have a red line going horizontally just like in the last question. That narrows our answer down to A and C. C doesn't have an arrow, but the arrow in A is going up instead of down like in the squares. A also has an additional red line, whereas C has the correct number of 3 blue lines and one red line. This means that C is the best answer even though it doesn't have an arrow. C is missing one thing (an arrow), but A has the arrow going the wrong way and has the incorrect color scheme.

Appendix B: Figure Matrices Answer Guide
Figure Matrices: Question 1

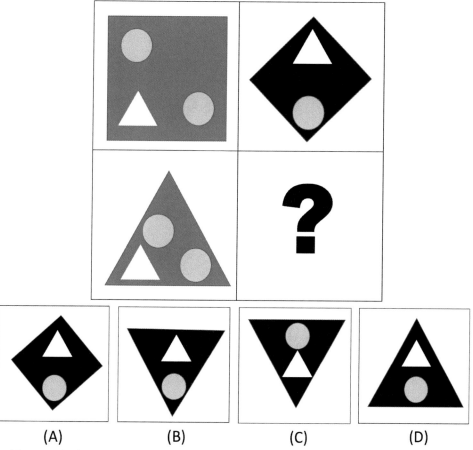

(A)   (B)   (C)   (D)

In this example the square rotates and turns black. Also, one of the yellow dots disappears. When we rotate the triangle, it will be pointing down with a dot on the bottom like in the top. The answer is B.

Figure Matrices: Question 2

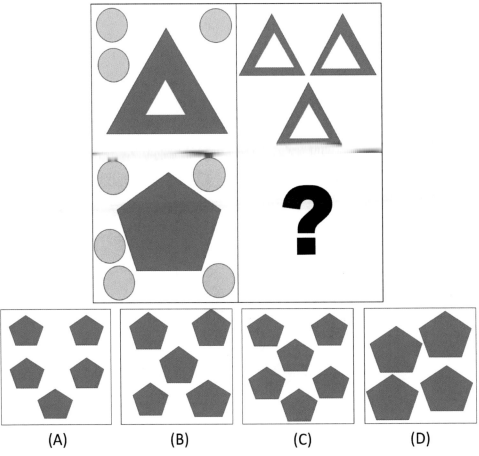

(A) (B) (C) (D)

All of the answers have a number of pentagons. How do we know how many pentagons we should have? The best information we have on the top is that we have 3 yellow dots, and then we end up with 3 triangles. We have 5 yellow dots on the bottom, so let's assume we should have 5 pentagons. That narrows down the answers to A or B. These answers are very similar, but A is a slightly better answer because the orientation of the pentagons more closely resembles the orientation of the triangles in the top row.

Figure Matrices: Question 3

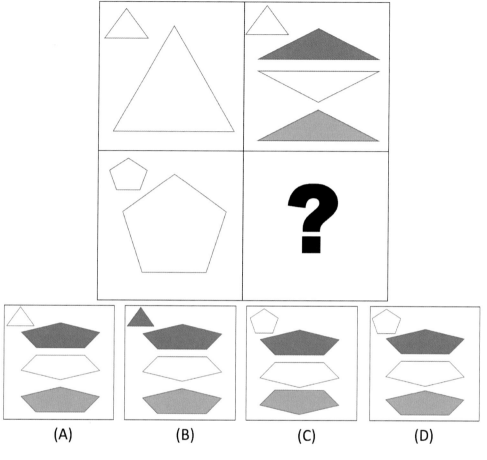

(A) (B) (C) (D)

The small triangle in the top left hand corner doesn't change in the example, so we can assume our answer will have a pentagon in the top left hand corner. That narrows down the answers to C or D. D is correct because in the example the green triangle points up; answer C has the pentagon pointing the wrong way.

Figure Matrices: Question 4

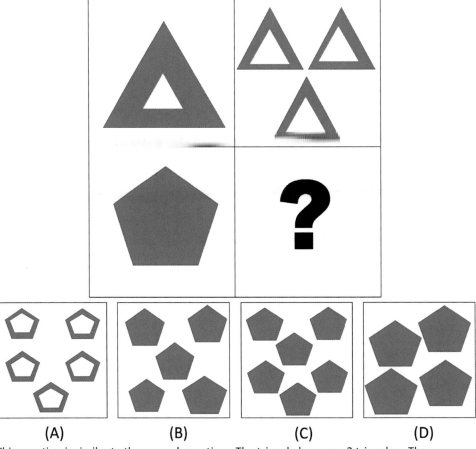

(A)　　　　(B)　　　　(C)　　　　(D)

This question is similar to the second question. The triangle becomes 3 triangles. The pentagon will turn into a number of pentagons. How many pentagons though? Looking for common numbers in the top two pictures. A Triangle has 3 sides and the top left triangle turned into 3 triangles in the top right picture. Apply this to the pentagon with 5 sides. The answer will be 5 pentagons. Answer B. A is not the answer because the white inner pentagons were not a part of the original image of the pentagon.

Figure Matrices: Question 5

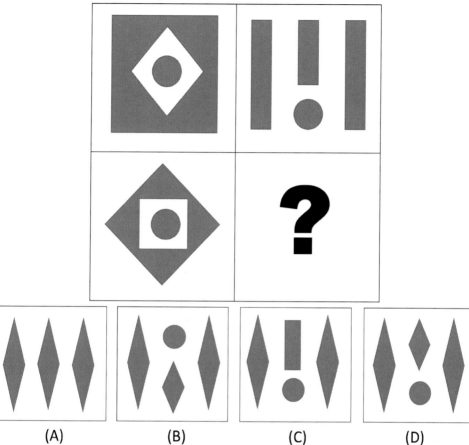

(A) (B) (C) (D)

The square turns in to 3 squished squares (rectangles) with a circle in the middle on the bottom. The white diamond on the top is just a distraction. On the bottom the diamond should turn in to 3 squished diamonds with a blue dot on the bottom center. D is the correct answer.

Figure Matrices: Question 6

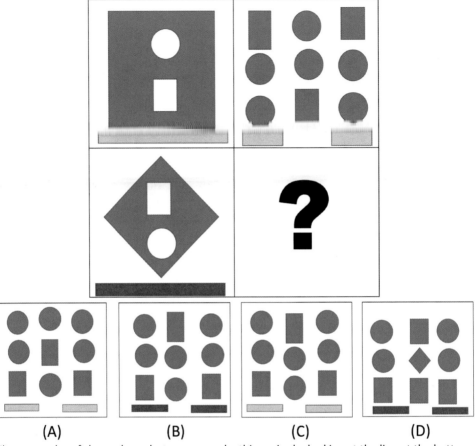

(A)   (B)   (C)   (D)

There are a lot of shapes here, but we can make this easier by looking at the line at the bottom first. We can tell that it is simply being turned in to 2 short lines of the same color, so on the bottom we have to have 2 small red lines. A and C are eliminated. D can be eliminated because of the center objects – it has a square on the top and the bottom which doesn't match. B is the correct answer.

Figure Matrices: Question 7

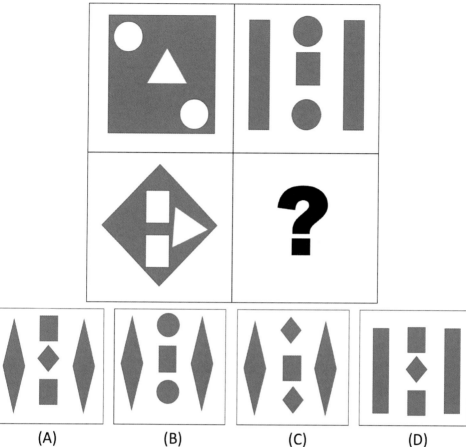

(A)   (B)   (C)   (D)

Right away we can tell that the triangle is being ignored at the top, and that the blue square goes to the sides and center. On the bottom, we can tell that the blue diamond is going to go to the sides and the center. A is the only answer that fits.

Figure Matrices: Question 8

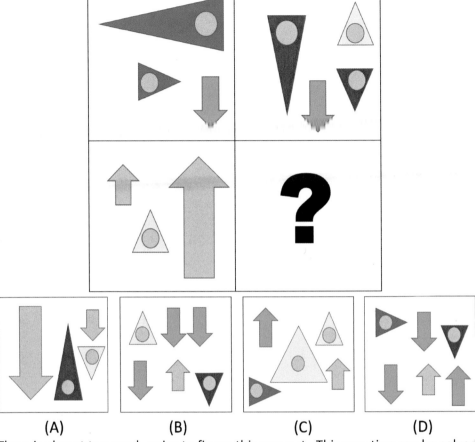

(A)   (B)   (C)   (D)

There is almost too much noise to figure this one out. This question can be solved more like a classification problem. We don't really know how this transformation is happening but we can see some common things. We can see green triangles are always pointed down. Orange are always pointed up. Red triangles are always down. Blue Triangles are pointed left or right... The only answer that has these all in common is answer B.

Figure Matrices: Question 9

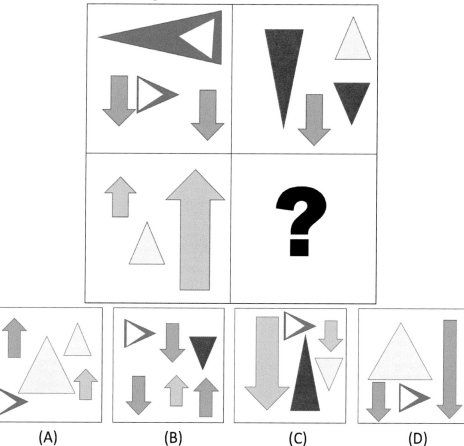

(A)   (B)   (C)   (D)

This one is solved in the same way as question 8. There is so much going on that finding a transformation is too hard. We just try to find a picture that looks most like the other ones. The top right picture especially is important with this method as it is the picture after the transformation. Answer D looks the most like the top right with green arrows pointing down and a yellow triangle pointing up. The blue triangle is noise either way as all answers have this.

Figure Matrices: Question 10

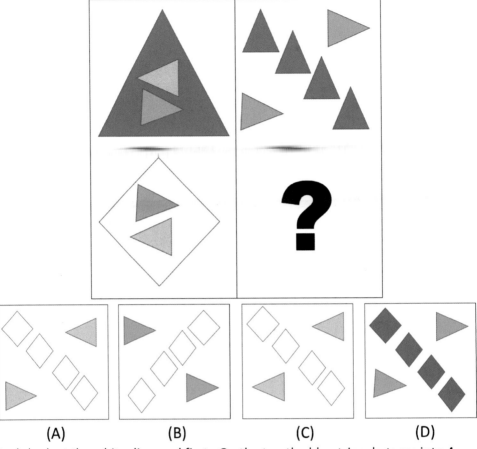

(A) (B) (C) (D)

Let's look at the white diamond first. On the top the blue triangle turns into 4 small triangles descending from top left to bottom right. B and D can be eliminated because they are going the wrong direction and are the wrong color. In the top squares, the green triangle is copied while the yellow triangle is ignored, on the bottom we should copy the bottom yellow triangle and ignore the green one. The yellow triangle points to the left so C is correct.

Figure Matrices: Question 11

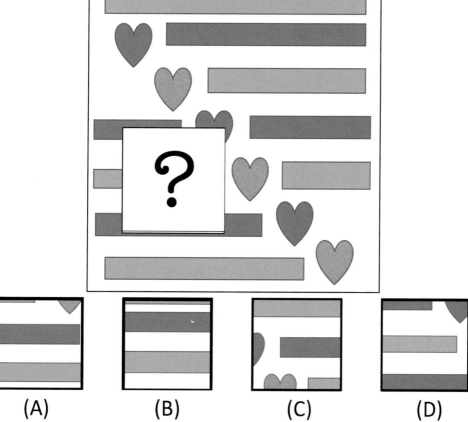

(A) (B) (C) (D)

We can see that the missing section should have part of a blue heart in the top right corner. D is the correct answer.

Figure Matrices: Question 12

(A)   (B)   (C)   (D)

Look at the right side of the square – we can see that it covers an entire column of circles and then part of another one. Only D can be correct because it is the only answer that includes an entire circle and part of one on the right side.

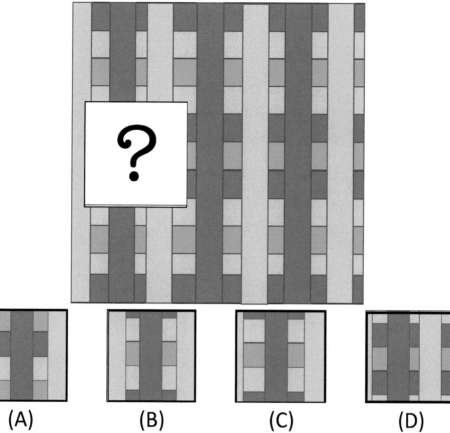

(A) (B) (C) (D)

Again let's look at the right side of the missing section. It contains the entire
vertical orange bar and then continues on past it a little bit. D must be correct
because it is the only answer that doesn't have an orange bar entirely on the right
side.

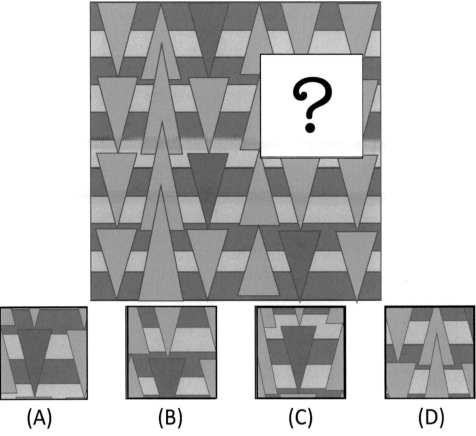

(A)   (B)   (C)   (D)

Look at the top of the missing section. We can see that it cuts off the tips of 2 triangles. Only A has the tips of 2 triangles at the top, so it is correct.

Figure Matrices: Question 15

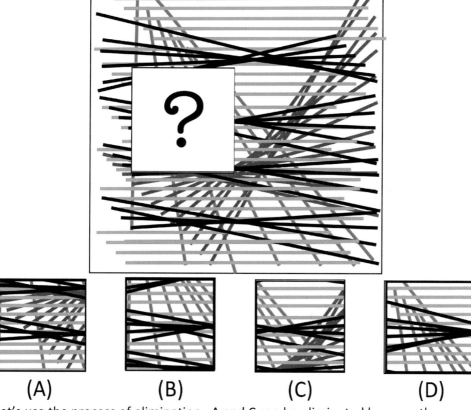

(A)　　　　　(B)　　　　　(C)　　　　　(D)

Let's use the process of elimination. A and C can be eliminated because they simply have far too many red lines in the wrong places. B and D look pretty similar, but if you look at the top you can tell there should be some black lines at the top of the answer. D is eliminated, and B is correct.

Figure Matrices: Question 16

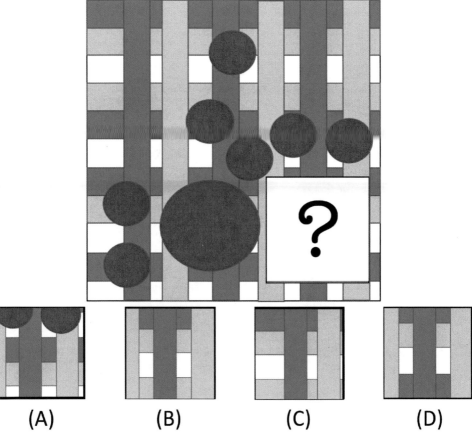

(A)   (B)   (C)   (D)

The important part of this question is to look at how the blue and orange lines are situated on top of each other and to track what color they are. We can see the vertical lines are on top of the horizontal ones and from left to right (behind the white box) it should go orange – blue – orange. The horizontal lines under it go blue – orange – white – blue. Answer D is the only answer with this pattern. Don't worry about the red dots, they are just noise.

Figure Matrices: Question 17

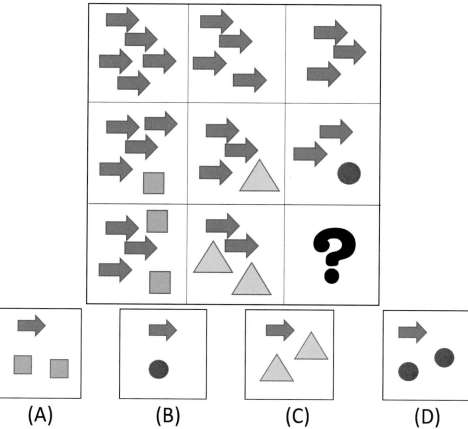

In the middle row we have a green square, then a yellow triangle, then a red dot. In the bottom row, we see the same color and shape pattern, but there are 2 of them instead of 1. Therefore, D is the correct answer because it has 2 red dots.

Figure Matrices: Question 18

(A)	(B)	(C)	(D)

In each row we start with 0 red, then 1, then 2. Also, the shapes turn red from the bottom up. A is correct because it has 2 red squares, and the red ones are on the bottom.

Figure Matrices: Question 19

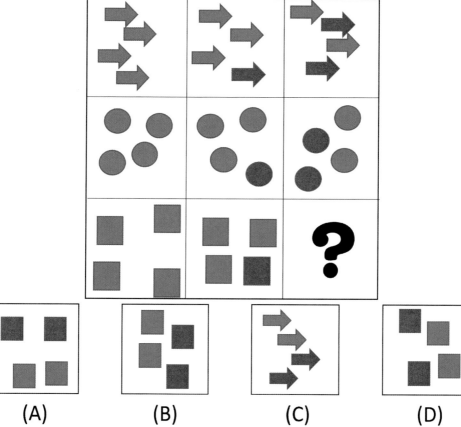

We know the shapes are turning red, but in what order? In the center column, the bottom shape turns red. In the third column, the red skips a shape so that the bottom shape and then the third from the bottom shape are red. B is correct because it matches this pattern.

Figure Matrices: Question 20

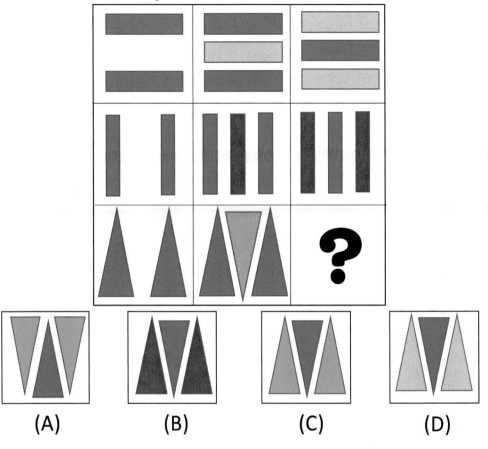

(A)   (B)   (C)   (D)

In the center row we see that the middle object turns red, and then the red moves to the 2 outside shapes. On the bottom, we can expect the green will move to the 2 outside shapes. C is the best answer because it is the same as the middle column, but the green has moved to the outside.

Figure Matrices: Question 21 (Bonus)

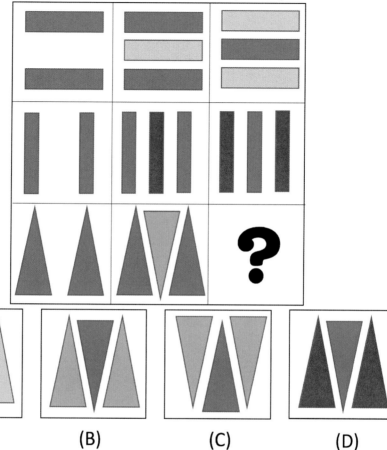

(A) (B) (C) (D)

In this question the color that is added in the second column then moves to the outsides in the third column. So we should expect green to be on the outsides. Is B or C correct? B is the best answer because we see that the triangles on the outsides stay pointing up.

Figure Matrices: Question 22 (Bonus)

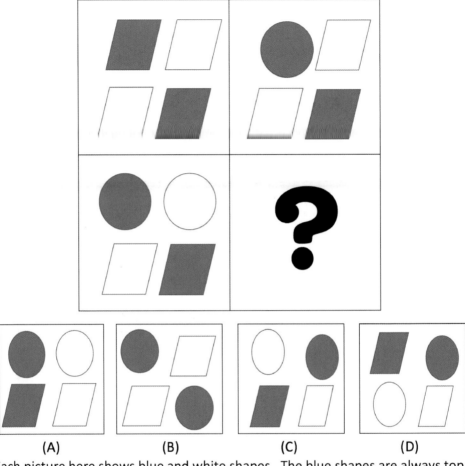

(A)   (B)   (C)   (D)

Each picture here shows blue and white shapes. The blue shapes are always top left and bottom right and the white shapes are always top right and bottom left. Answer B is the only one with this characteristic.

The idea that there may be 0, 1 or 2 circles is just there to throw you off the real answer.

Figure Matrices: Question 23 (Bonus)

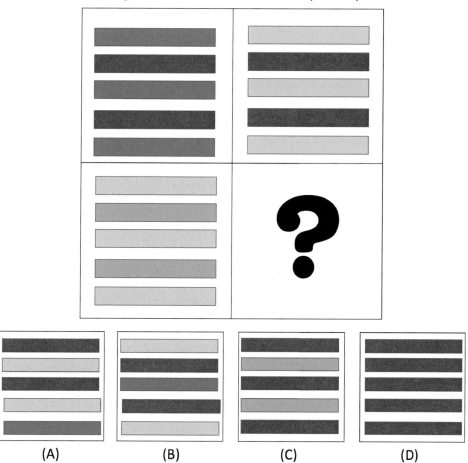

(A)   (B)   (C)   (D)

Each shape presented has exactly two colors and the colors alternate from one to the other. Kind of like boy-girl-boy-girl seating. Answer C is the only answer that has two colors that alternate.

Figure Matrices: Question 24 (Bonus)

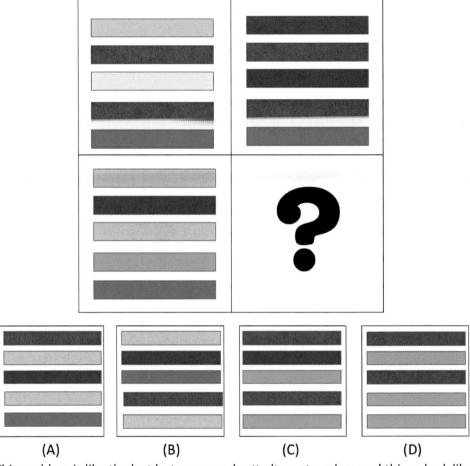

(A)   (B)   (C)   (D)

This problem is like the last but now we don't alternate colors and things look like a mess.

Investigate each shape and ask yourself "What is similar among these shapes?"

Each shape has a blue line on the bottom. Answer A has a blue line on the bottom, all other answers do not.

It is ok to struggle with this one. You are training to drown out the noise and try to find what is important to each picture.

Figure Matrices: Question 25 (Bonus)

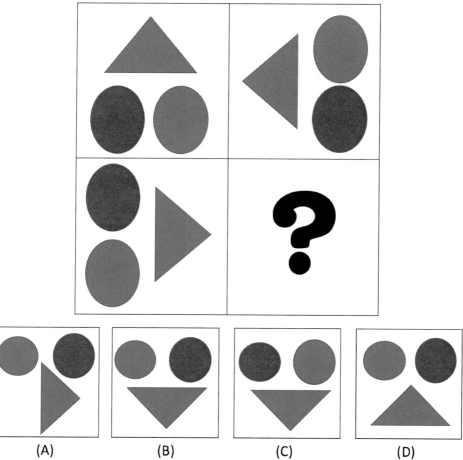

(A)   (B)   (C)   (D)

Ok you should recognize these shapes from a previous question. This time though we have introduced red shapes into the mix. The answer is B. Can you figure out why? Let's do elimination. In each sample the triangle points away from the circles. Answer A and D are out!

So we have left B and C which only look different in where the red circle is placed. To figure this out take any one of the pictures presented and 'rotate' the whole picture so that the triangle is pointing down. When you do this you should see the red circle should be on the right side when the triangle is pointing down.

Answer C is out and Answer B is the winner.

Paper Folding: Question 1

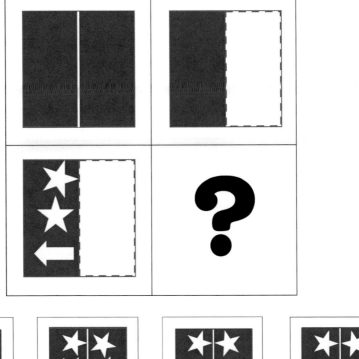

(A)

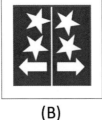
(B)

(C)

(D)

When we unfold the paper, the arrow will be pointing the opposite way. That narrows down our answer to B or C. B is incorrect because the bottom star is tilted, while in the question it shows that the bottom star is straight. C is correct.

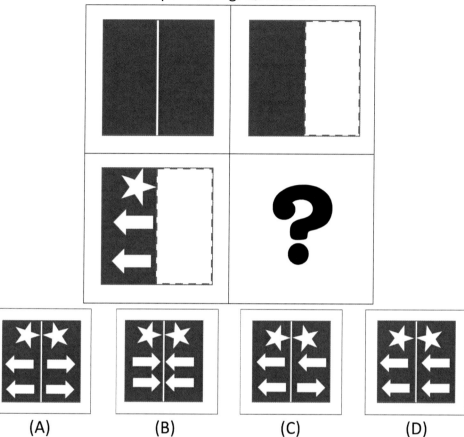

(A)   (B)   (C)   (D)

When we unfold the paper, the arrows will face the opposite direction. That means that A must be correct, because it is the only one that has arrows pointing opposite directions while maintaining the initial position on the left.

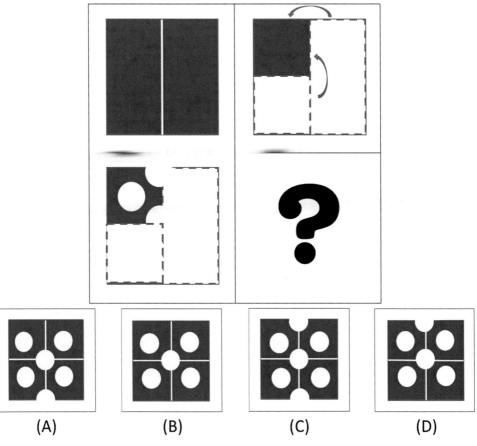

(A) (B) (C) (D)

When we unfold this paper, we can expect a half circle at the top and bottom. We also should have a circle right in the middle of the paper. C is the correct answer because it has the half circles at the top and bottom.

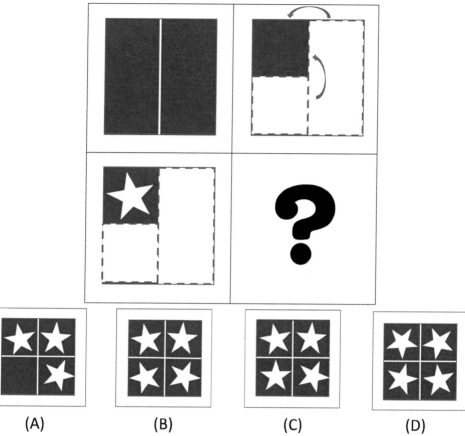

(A)   (B)   (C)   (D)

When we unfold this star horizontally, the star on the right should be tilted the opposite way as the initial star. The initial star is tilted up on the right side with a point towards the center of the paper. The next star will be tilted up on the left side with a point towards the center. The final unfold will reveal two more stars with points towards the center of the paper. Answer B is the best choice.

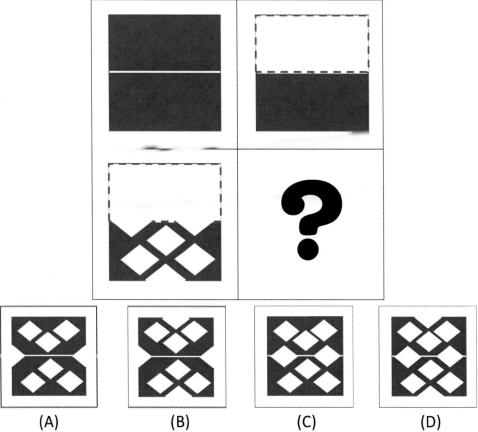

(A)   (B)   (C)   (D)

There are a lot of shapes here, so let's use the process of elimination. We can eliminate A and B because of the half diamonds in the center left and right. Those half diamonds don't exist. Between C and D, D must be correct because of the half diamond at the bottom and the top center.

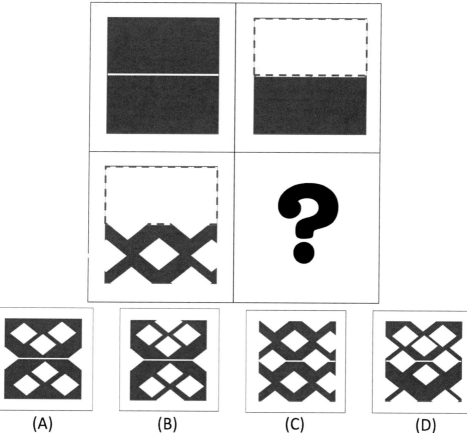

(A)   (B)   (C)   (D)

Like in the last question, we can eliminate A and B because of the half diamond in the center left and right. C is the correct answer because of the spacing of the diamonds; D has inconsistent spacing. Some spaces are too tiny and some are too big.

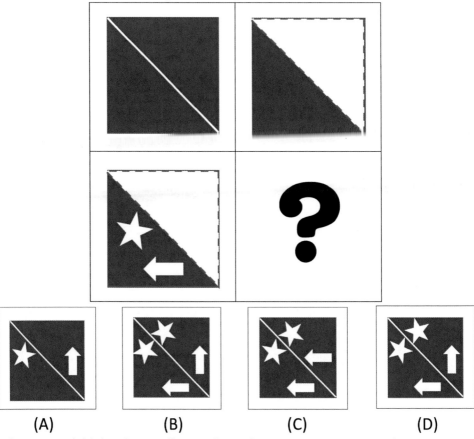

(A)   (B)   (C)   (D)

When we unfold this diagonally, it will put the arrow pointing up. This narrows down our possible answers to B or D. B and D are very similar, but if you look closely you will see that the star on the left in B does not match the star in the initial picture; it slightly rotates to its right. That means D is the correct answer.

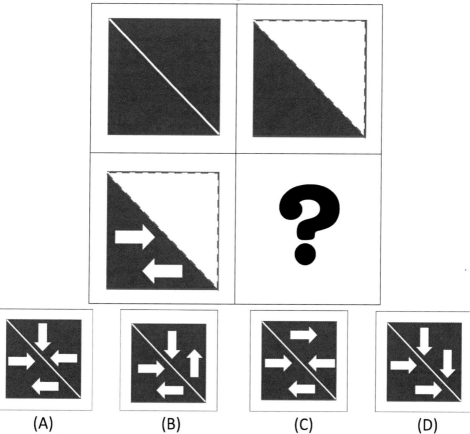

(A)   (B)   (C)   (D)

Just like in the last question, the bottom arrow will end up pointing straight up. B is the only answer that has this, so it must be correct.

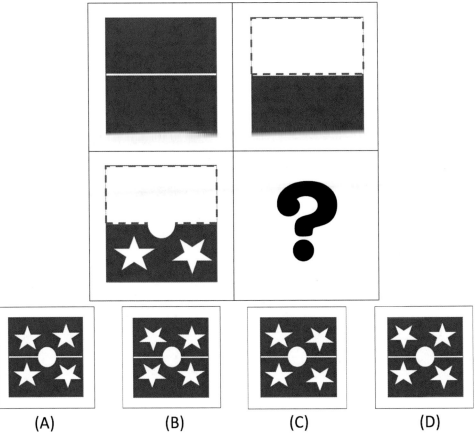

| (A) | (B) | (C) | (D) |

In this question we will be looking at how the stars are rotated. The left star is straight up and down and has a point pointing straight up. That means when it is flipped it will have a point pointing straight down. That narrows it down to B and D. B can't be right because the stars on the bottom don't match the question, which means that D is correct.

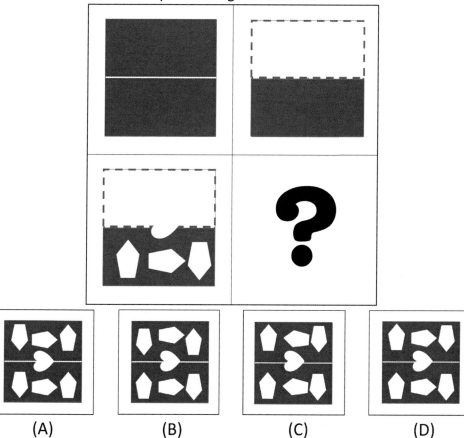

(A) (B) (C) (D)

For this question, focus on the shapes pointing up and down. When unfolded, they will face the opposite direction. The question has the left one pointing up and the right one pointing down, which means the answer should have the left one pointing down and the right one pointing up. A is the correct answer.

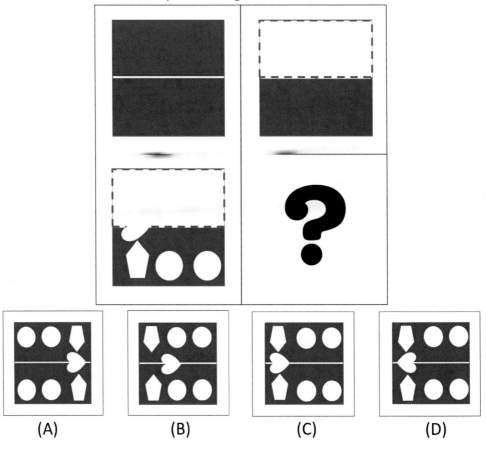

(A)   (B)   (C)   (D)

The pointed shape needs to face the opposite direction, and the heart needs to be lined up with it vertically. B is wrong because the heart isn't lined up, and D is wrong because the heart is pointed the wrong way. C is the correct answer.

Paper Folding: Question 12

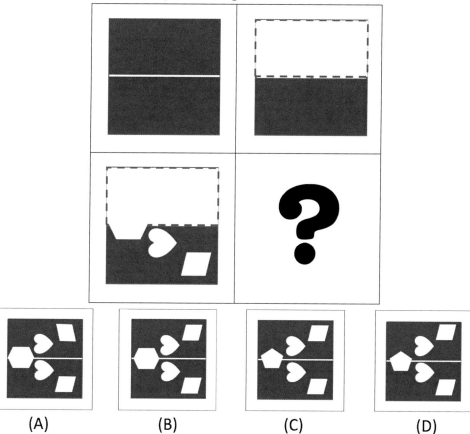

(A)   (B)   (C)   (D)

The 3-sided shape that is split on the center line should turn into a 6-sided shape. That eliminates C and D. The 4-sided shape needs to be flipped upside down. Answer B has the same exact 4-sided shape on the top and bottom, which means it is incorrect. That leaves A as the correct answer.

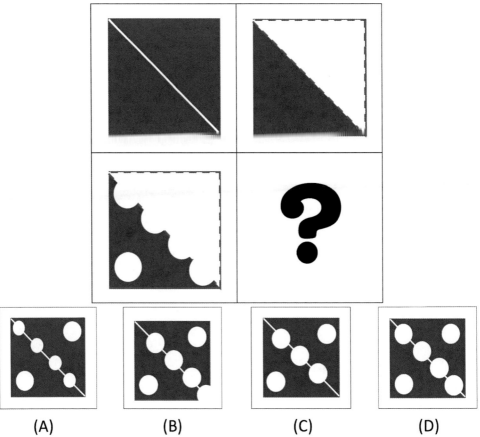

(A)   (B)   (C)   (D)

When we unfold this paper diagonally, we should have 4 circles going down the middle. A is eliminated because the circles are too small. B is eliminated because the circles are slid down too far to the bottom right. C is eliminated because it only has 3 circles. D is the only one left.

Paper Folding: Question 14

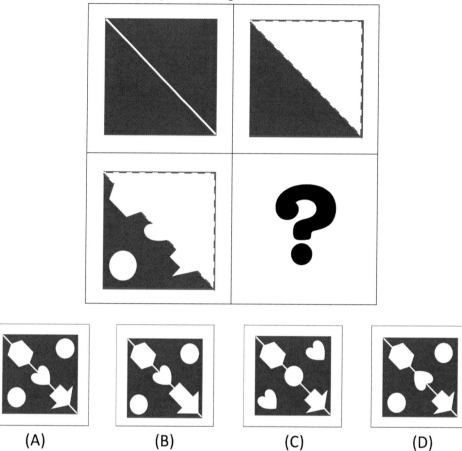

(A)   (B)   (C)   (D)

Just focus on the circle and the heart. The circle should be in the top right when the paper is unfolded. That eliminates C. D has the heart going the wrong way, so it is also eliminated. Between A and B, the arrow in B is simply too big. That means A is the correct answer.

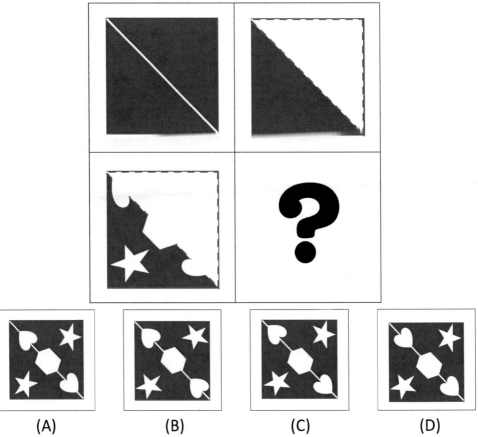

(A) (B) (C) (D)

If we look at the hearts first, we can see that we need to have the hearts pointing to the outside. That means A or C is the correct answer. It is hard to tell which one is correct, but if you look closely you will see that in A the initial star doesn't match the question. That means C is the correct answer.

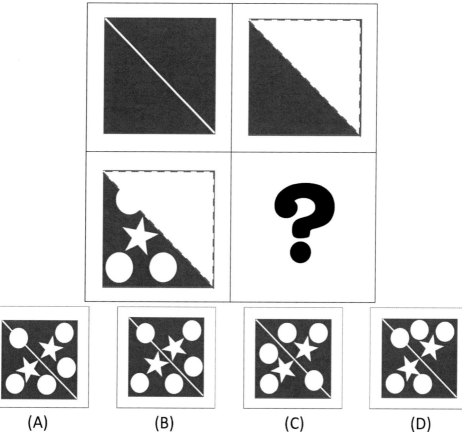

(A)   (B)   (C)   (D)

The 2 circles on the bottom will end up on the right side when we unfold it. That means the answer is A or B. The star in A doesn't match the orientation of the star in the question, which means that B is the correct answer.

Appendix D: Number Series Tips

A number series is a sequence of numbers that have a logical pattern. In this section we will train you up on some tips on how to recognize the pattern and find the best answer.

Let's start easy, can you identify the next number?

$$1 \quad 2 \quad 3 \quad 4 \quad \_\_\_\_\_$$

The next number is of course 5. Why do you know that it is 5 though? You know it is 5 because you can tell that you are counting by 1, or always doing + 1.

When you do harder patterns, you can sometimes still ask yourself, "What number am I adding each time?" Try this one:

$$1 \quad 3 \quad 5 \quad 7 \quad \_\_\_\_\_$$

The next number is 9. This time you were just thinking "+2" after each number.

Now try this:

$$1 \quad 1 \quad 2 \quad 3 \quad 5 \quad 8 \quad \_\_\_\_\_$$

If you said the next number is 11 then you would be wrong. The correct answer is 12. In this example, we aren't adding the same number each time, so you have to remind yourself to always check the whole pattern. We are actually always adding the previous 2 numbers together to get the next number. This is a common pattern you need to recognize in math. So the pattern goes 1 + nothing is still 1, giving you your first 2 numbers 1 1. Then 1 + 1 = 2, so now your pattern is 1 1 2. Then 1 + 2 = 3 so now are pattern is 1 1 2 3. Then 2 + 3 = 5, and 3 + 5 = 8, giving us the whole pattern of 1 1 2 3 5 8. To get the next number, we add the previous 2 numbers, so we do 5 + 8 = 13, which is the correct answer.

Number series can also use subtraction:

$$10 \quad 8 \quad 6 \quad 4 \quad \underline{\hspace{2em}}$$

In this example what number are we always subtracting? The answer is - 2.

Number series can double:

$$1 \quad 2 \quad 4 \quad 8 \quad \underline{\hspace{2em}}$$

Each time the number doubles, which means it is added to itself. The next number would be 8 + 8 which means the answer is 16. If we did the next number after that it would be 16 + 16 = 32.

Sequences can divide:

$$40 \quad 20 \quad 10 \quad \underline{}$$

Each time the number is divided in half. To get half of a number, you have to figure out what number can be added to itself to get the answer. So our last number in this pattern is 10, what number can be added to itself to get 10? Think of it like this: ? + ? = 10? The answer is 5.

Number series can sometimes just be a pattern; there might not be any math at all:

$$1 \quad\quad 12 \quad\quad 123 \quad\quad \underline{}$$

There is no real addition going on here. The sequence just adds the next number in the number line to it. "To get the next number add another digit on the end. This digit will be one more than the last digit in the previous number." The next number would be 1234, then 12345, then 123456 …

Let's try some more tricks:

$$1 \quad 0 \quad 2 \quad 0 \quad 3 \quad 0 \quad \underline{}$$

The next number is 4. The alternating 0's are just noise to throw you off the trail. Our statement is "Add one to the last number that WASN'T a 0."

10 01 20 02 30 _____

"The next number will either be the next 10 in the series of 10's OR it will flip the tens and ones place." The last number was 30 so the next number will be 03. The next few will be 40, 04, 50, 05 …

0001   0010   0100   _____

Binary anyone? "To get the next number move the 1 left by one place." The next number is 1000.

More Practice:

40   4   30   3   20   _____

6   6   5   5   4   _____

12   10   8   6   _____

40   35   30   25   20   _____

11   13   15   17   _____

3   6   9   12   15   _____

6   5   65   4   5   _____

7   6   7   6   7   _____

5 10 15 20 25 _____

8 6 4 2 _____

Answers:

40 4 30 3 20 2

6 6 5 5 4 4

12 10 8 6 4

40 35 30 25 20 15

11 13 15 17 19

3 6 9 12 15 18

6 5 65 4 5 45

(see we joined the 6 and the 5 to make 65? Now we join the 4 and 5 to make 45)

7 6 7 6 7 6

5 10 15 20 25 30

8 6 4 2 0

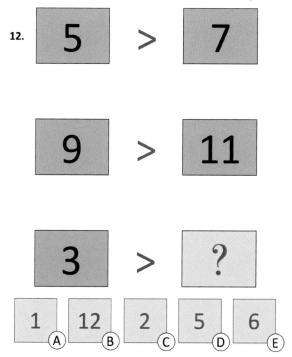

12.

The number puzzles could be seen as miniature pieces of a number sequence. You are given 2 sets of numbers and you are told to figure out how they relate, then select an answer to fit the third set of numbers.

Above there are two samples:

5 turns to 7
9 turns to 11

Our logic statement "Take the number on the left and add 2 to it." Our number 3 will turn into 5. (Answer D)

The real work here is finding out how the two numbers on the left turn into the two numbers on the right and then do that same thing to the third number on the bottom.

All of the changes in number puzzles will be addition, subtraction, multiplication or division. Multiplication and division will be limited to things like doubling or halving.

Let's practice identifying how numbers change:

$$2 \rightarrow 4$$
$$4 \rightarrow 6$$

"Add 2 to the number on the left to get the number on the right" If our third number were 100 then you would look for the answer that was 100 + 2.

Try this:

$$2 \rightarrow 4$$
$$4 \rightarrow 8$$

This one looks the same but it is multiplication based. We are doubling the number. Don't be hasty! If you just looked at the first set and said "Ok $2 \rightarrow 4$, we are adding 2 to each number on the left." You'd be wrong. The lesson is to take in all of the information presented and then make your decision.

Try this:

$$10 \rightarrow 5$$
$$8 \rightarrow 4$$

"Divide the left number in half to get the right number"

And this:

$$15 \rightarrow 9$$
$$20 \rightarrow 14$$

"Subtract 6 from the number on the left"

More Practice:

$$15 \rightarrow 20$$
$$0 \rightarrow 5$$

$$6 \rightarrow 12$$
$$5 \rightarrow 10$$

$$8 \rightarrow 4$$
$$7 \rightarrow 3.5$$
$$6 \rightarrow 3$$

$$21 \rightarrow 7$$
$$6 \rightarrow 2$$

$$0 \rightarrow 4$$
$$7 \rightarrow 11$$

$$7 \rightarrow 4$$
$$15 \rightarrow 12$$

Answers:

15→20
0→5
"Add 5 to the number on the left"

6→12
5→10
"Double the number on the left"

8→4
7→3.5
6→3
"Divide the number on the left in half"

21→7
6→2
"Divide the number on the left into 3 parts" or
"Divide the number on the left by 3"

0→4
7→11
"Add 4 to the number on the left"

7→4
15→12
"Subtract 3 from the number on the left"

Appendix F: Critical Thinking, Testing Tips & Exercises

Have you ever been sold on testing tips or seen testing tips as a part of the advertised education product to only see the tired list of "Be sure to eat a good breakfast!" and "Get a good night sleep!"? Well aside from quoting those worn out phrases we will not push this on you. We have actual words of wisdom to work out.

These are best served as conversation pieces or action items to be taken one or two in a sitting. Each page will have its own topic of discussion, feel free to skip around.

Appendix F: Critical Thinking, Testing Tips & Exercises

What is Critical Thinking?

Critical thinking is taking information into your brain, **processing the information** and using the processed information to make better decisions.

What does that mean to "process the information"? For our purposes in the test we are mostly talking about the logic that is happening when you try to solve a problem. When looking at three shapes and trying to determine how they are similar there is a logical **loop of questions** that plays out:

"Are the shapes the same color?"
"Do the shapes have the same number of sides?"
"Do the shapes point the same way?"

Processing information can also come from the student's past experience, beliefs, or other reasoning skills.

When you want to train to win the test you have to think of how you are going to process information. Then given a question type what is your loop of questions?

The next pages go into more detail on these concepts.

Appendix F: Critical Thinking, Testing Tips & Exercises

The Loop of Questions and Training Habit

A morning routine may look like this: Wake up, brush your teeth, take a shower, get dressed, eat breakfast, leave the house.

This is a cycle of actions that is taken every day and very little actual thought must be taken since it is a habit. The same idea needs to be applied to the sections of the test. You see a question and you have a list of questions to help **process the information**.

Look at these number sequences:

5	10	15	20	25
10	11	12	13	14
8	6	4	2	0

Each of these shows a different pattern but the loop of questions is the same:

"Are we adding across the sequence?"
"Are we subtracting across the sequence?"
"Are we multiplying across the sequence?"
"Are we dividing across the sequence?"

Action: On an index card develop a set of questions for each question type in this book and practice using your loop of questions. Feel free to add questions to your card as you work through the problems.

Appendix F: Critical Thinking, Testing Tips & Exercises
You Tell Me! Creating Your Own Test

Nothing helps critical thinking like having the student create their own problems. Have the student use this drawing as a template to create logic problems like the visual sections in this book.

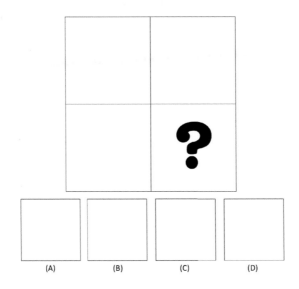

Action: Have the student create a set of problems for you to solve on scratch paper. The questions must be logical and they must be able to explain the correct answer and why the other answers are not correct.

Bonus: Have the student create other types of questions like number strings and number puzzles.

a) 5	b) 6	c) 7	d) 8	e) 9

Appendix F: Critical Thinking, Testing Tips & Exercises

Question Each Answer

The test is asking you questions. Turn the tables and ask questions of the test! Here we want to find the right picture to fit the bottom right block. Let's have an imaginary conversation

You: "Answer A-D Why are you not the correct answer?"
Answer A: "I'm a blue diamond with a green arrow pointing diagonally. I am in the third column where all arrows point down. I am probably not the answer"
Answer B: "I have a green arrow that points down. I am pointing the right way but each row has the third arrow the same color as the first arrow. I should be red"
Answer C: "I am a red arrow pointing down, I may be the right answer"
Answer D: "I am a yellow arrow pointing down, I am not the right answer"

Action: Try questioning answers with a few practice problems in each section.

Appendix F: Critical Thinking, Testing Tips & Exercises

Test Each Answer

Similar to question each answer, we will now test each answer. This is a very powerful tool in acing any type of multiple choice algebra type test.

Look at this number series

$$4 \quad 5 \quad 45 \quad 6 \quad 7 \quad \underline{\quad}$$

A) 7   B)8   C)21   D) 4   E)67

This looks like a simple addition, add each number to the last. But what is that 45 in the middle of the string for? Well test each answer and see if it looks like it can fit mentally place each answer into the space and see if it looks right. Answer E is correct. Once placed in the answer spot you may "see the pattern" 4 and 5 become 45; 6 and 7 become 67!

Look at this Number Puzzle

a) 7   b) 6   c) 5   d) 8   e) 9

Substitute the triangle for the 4 and write the problem as 4 + 3 on your scratch paper. Now we have 4 + 3 = ? Replace the answers presented to see which one fits the problem. 4 + 3 = 7? Yes, the answer is A.

Appendix F: Critical Thinking, Testing Tips & Exercises

Mental Gymnastics for Attention to Detail

In grade school you are given a sheet of math, it may have 5 or 10 of the same type of problem. Maybe you get 10 addition and 10 subtraction problems. You do the 10 addition problems, then do the 10 subtraction problems. Your ability to pay attention to detail is slightly dropped as you work through 10 of the same type of problem. You don't have to think "Oh this is an addition problem...what are the rules for addition?...ok time to do addition." You know all 10 are addition so you work them like an assembly line.

Action: Instead of working 10 of the same type of problem work one problem from each of the 9 sets in this book. The process of switching problem types after each problem forces you to examine the rule set.

"Ok it's a number series, in these the series could be addition, subtraction, multiplication or division."

"Ok it's picture categories and I need to look for similar shapes, counts, colors, sides and so on."

Appendix F: Critical Thinking, Testing Tips & Exercises

Proverbs for Exercising Analysis Skills

Define Analysis: examination of something. Breaking complicated things into smaller parts to gain understanding.

Analysis is determining the intended meaning of some bit of information. When you analyze pictures for categories you are breaking the pictures into smaller parts to understand them. "Does each picture have a triangle?" is a good analysis question.

Here we will recognize your analysis skills by discussing proverbs. A proverb is a simple saying that has a deeper meaning. First break the proverb into parts, try to understand the parts and then guess at the overall meaning.

Have the student tell you what each of these proverbs means after their careful analysis.

"The early bird gets the worm."

"There is more to knowing than just being correct."

"A book holds a house of gold."

"A diamond with a flaw is worth more than a perfect pebble."

"Deep doubts, deep wisdom; small doubts, little wisdom."

"Dig the water well before you are thirsty."

This concludes our book. Be sure to check out our COGAT® Trainer apps on iTunes and Google Play. Just search for COGAT® Trainer and look for Polemics Applications.

Visit us at www.polemicsmath.com we have a growing community of parents and educators and lots of free blog content on gifted and talented testing.

Send all feedback to info@polemicsmath.com

Polemics Math

Made in the USA
Columbia, SC
27 October 2021

47911054R10113